# SURVIVING SUMMERS WITH KIDS

## Funfilled Activities for All

---

*Make Wonderful memories!*

### RITA B. HERRON

*Rita B Herron*

*Illustrations by Clyde Carver*

**R&E Publishers** • **Saratoga, California**

**R & E Publishers**
P.O. Box 2008, Saratoga, CA 95070
Tel: (408) 866-6303    Fax: (408) 866-0825

*Book Design by Diane Parker*
*Front Cover and Illustrations by Clyde Carver*

Library of Congress Card Catalog Number: 93-2275

ISBN 1-56875-052-8

# CONTENTS

# THE LOOKING GLASS

*by Rita Herron*

If only we held a looking glass
In which we could gently see
The hours of time beneath us
And all that we wished could be.

The hint of tiny laughter
The pain of young one's tears
The trusting hand within ours
Grows timely throughout the years.

But when the moment has passed us by
We sadly turn to see
The looking glass was standing there
And all that we wished could be.

# DEDICATION

To my three beautiful and wonderful children
who provided me with the inspiration
and understanding to write this book.

# DEDICATION

With special thanks to:

- My three children Adam, Elizabeth, and Emily, whose hugs I could not live without and who drove me crazy enough to write this book.

- My husband Lee, who through his model of perseverance and a positive outlook on life taught me to persevere, who patiently taught me, the machine illiterate, how to use a computer, who doesn't allow me to sit on the pity pot too long when something goes wrong, and for making me believe that anything is possible.

- My mother Ellen, who struggled and gave up much to raise me, who gave me the stubbornness and strong will to survive, and who taught me to appreciate the simple things in life like a good glass of cornbread and milk.

- My twin sister Reba, who understands me as only a twin can, has PMS as bad as I do, who counseled me through mailbox phobia and rejections, and who encouraged me to stop watching soap operas and do something with my life.

- My brother Marcus, who gave me the strength and determination to go to college against financial odds, whose "illusions of grandeur" I acquired, and who gave me my first ride in a convertible.

- My best friend Nancy, who attempted to have conversation and a cup of coffee with me when our babies were small and our boobs were big (from nursing), who laughs when she's suppose to at my books, listens when she should, especially to all the petty and unimportant things I have to say, and cries at the same things I do.

- My close friend Patsy, whose background was akin to mine, and who supported me by offering to sell my books in her store, Parsons Hallmark of Duluth, Georgia, even if they sold no where else.

- My friend Kathy, who told me I was a genius when I knew I wasn't but needed to hear it.

- All my friends and co-teachers at the Duluth First Baptist Preschool, for their undying support through fingerpainting, glue, crazy art projects, my midlife crisis and my decision to write.

- All the mothers in the world who suffer through pregnancy, labor and delivery and then have the courage to do it again, who give up small luxury cars to drive taxi cabs and who know that the pleasure and the rewards for raising a child are invisible to the naked eye.

- All the fathers in the world who are now more involved in their children's lives, who have accepted that Donna Reed was only a fairy tale in history, and who have ever camped out all night in order to make sure their child got a spot on the community little league team.

- All the children in the world, who through muddy shoes and grass stained clothes give us something to live for: laundry.

- All my teachers throughout the years, who inspired me to follow in their footsteps, even if the salary couldn't pay for my kids' shoes. My next book is dedicated to you. Look for it soon!

- Pete Seger, for the beautiful song he wrote "Where Have All the Flowers Gone" and the many meanings it has to all.

- And special thanks to Mr. Bob Reed for making this book possible and for believing in first time authors!

# INTRODUCTION
## SURVIVING SUMMERS
## WITH KIDS
### Yes, It Can Be Done!

You may be doubtful. You may be anxious. You may even be chewing your fingernails and mumbling obscenities, but yes, the summer can be survived with minimal damage to your psyche, only occasional therapy (okay, daily) from your friends and perhaps only a minute weight gain or loss (depending on your personal body's reaction to stress). Yes, it can be done. All you need to do is use a little bit of careful planning and thought. After all, a soldier wouldn't go to war without his weapons, a swimmer wouldn't dive into the pool without holding his breath, and a jogger wouldn't run a marathon without warming up. Certainly we should not compare being at home with our beloved children to any of the above, because we all know summer is wonderful, fun, lazy, and relaxing, (or it use to be in the BC 32 years, before children). If you are lucky enough to be at home with your children for the summer, you probably have chosen to do so and in your heart you really love it. You know this time is precious and rewarding and that you are making memories that will last forever with your children. But let's face it, even the most wonderful days of our lives, the best intentions, and the best laid plans fall prey to the stresses of everyday life with children. Your idealism may find itself dwindling when fatigue, dirty laundry, and an irritable child decide to test your limits. One child needing a nap, a sudden onset fever, the neighborhood gang dropping in, twenty-five empty cups sitting on your counter and the other millions of trivial upsets during one day can force you to look for measures to save your own sanity. Of course, if you are a working mother by choice or necessity, your feelings may be similar but you also face a different plight; a special section is devoted just to you so please read on.

So, moms, take a few minutes for yourself, read a chapter a day, say your prayers, and tell yourself ten times: SURVIVING SUMMERS WITH KIDS: YES, IT CAN BE DONE!

# CHAPTER 1
## HURRAH! SCHOOL'S OUT:
## NOW WHAT?

It's finally here! The last day of school! You and the kids have been counting the days: longing for those lazy days of summer when you can sleep late, sit by the pool, read, relax, invite friends over for cookouts, and forget about the carpools.

The last few hectic months filled with busy schedules, meals from paper bags handed to you by strangers through tiny glass windows, late nights at ballparks, dirty bodies and hair to wash at midnight, dragging tired children from their beds, eating cold cereal and rushing for the bus, recitals, spring cleaning, yardwork, meetings, and programs, endless running around; yes, it's finally coming to a close. Now you can actually sit down, take a breath, sip your morning coffee, even savor a second cup instead of drinking it in the car, read the paper, take long blissful strolls with the family and perhaps gain control over your crazy life. You have ached for these precious moments to come. You have visions of preparing fresh fruits and five course dinners. You picture the entire family eating together, sharing and laughing and talking. You're going to finally invite all those friends over that your good intentions haven't had time for. You can try new recipes, finish the project (whatever your hobby is) that you began last summer, and have time to shop and lunch with friends.

You're not sure why, but as the school parties end, a tinge of sadness creeps in. Then as the children drag in book bags overflowing with school papers, left over school supplies, and moldy lunch boxes, you suddenly feel a wave of unexplained panic. You immediately search for cover as the mounds of broken crayons, shattered pencils, erasers, torn papers, left over cheetos, and the bird nest your child took for show and tell four months ago are emptied onto the den floor.

"Why don't we go through all these things, choose a few special papers to keep, and throw the rest away, sweetheart. You know we just don't have room for all of them. Okay?" You smile sweetly, speaking in your most patient voice.

"No, Mommy," your child screeches, "I want to keep them all. Then I can play school with them all summer." You watch in awe as your child quickly scoops up as much of the mess as he can carry and marches upstairs. Of course, he leaves a tiny trail of crumbs, torn paper, and half inch long pencil stubs behind.

With no warning, the ham sandwich you ate for lunch turns to knots in your stomach. You sink into the big arm chair letting out a small sigh. You check your watch, 4:45. For a second you contemplate the cold beer in the fridge. It's almost 5:00 you tell yourself. No, you decide, you've been longing for this day for months. Relax, enjoy the children, you order yourself.

The phone rings, another salesman. The doorbell rings and in walk five of the neighborhood children. You hear shouting voices at the top of the stairs, "Mommy, he's staring at me!" "Well, she looked at me first!" "He says I can't play." A voice calls from the bathroom, "Mom, can you bring me some toilet paper! There's none in here." You grab a roll from the downstairs bath and climb the steps. You try to turn the knob but the door is locked. "Honey, you're going to have to unlock the door," you say. "But I can't get up!" he cries. "Darling, Mommy can't give you the tissue unless you unlock the door." You hear sobs and the sliding of feet. The door cracks open slightly as the phone rings again. You toss the paper inside and run for the phone. It's your husband, "Hi, Honey, what's for dinner?"

You suddenly burst into laughter. To laugh or to cry; you had to choose. "We're ordering pizza," you tell your husband, head for the other bathroom, shut the door, stare at yourself in the mirror and hear yourself say, "HURRAH! SCHOOL'S OUT, NOW WHAT?"

# 9:30 A.M. MORNING ONE— HELP! I'M CALLING A BABYSITTER!

You know you remember physically dragging the kids out of bed those last few weeks at 7:30. You dressed them in their sleep, then watched them change as they woke up and argued with you about the clothes you had picked out. You prodded them to walk down the steps and forced them to eat at least five bites of their cereal because as a good mother you couldn't survive the guilt of knowing you sent your child to school on an empty stomach. With these memories in mind, you're confident that everyone is looking forward to sleeping late and being couch potatoes on this first morning of summer break. But morning one arrives, and at 6:15 a.m. you roll over in your bed to find lots of bodies keeping you company. The kids, the new kittens, they're all on top of you. You cringe under the covers as they bounce up and down on the bed and crawl on your face. You wave them to leave, mumbling, "Go downstairs." Then you hear them race down the steps, giggling and squealing. Have they already had candy bars this morning? You ask yourself this as you roll over quickly, trying not to let your body get too awake. You slowly fade back to sleep, relying on the tube to keep them entertained while you doze (something you swore you would never encourage in the B.C. years; before children), but three children later and numerous hours and nights of lost sleep have mellowed your views, at least temporarily.

Sweet dreams overcome you momentarily but as the clock approaches 7:00, you hear thunder and the patter of rain on the roof. Next comes the explosion downstairs. Screams and tears fill the air and seep into your room. Your feet instantly hit the floor. You find yourself charging down the steps two at a time to settle the first battle of the day while you try to bottle your anger and remind yourself that it is summer, your special time with your children.

You shovel cereal into bowls as someone reminds you that you promised pancakes when school was out. "Tomorrow," you mutter as you crawl onto the couch clutching your coffee. You're still determined to salvage a little of the morning for your dream. You hear the familiar tune to "Bewitched," one of your favorite old shows (okay, we all get stuck somewhere in one of our childhood stages). You savor every sip from your morning fix as you settle into the reruns. You run your fingers around the rim of your cup letting the aroma of the coffee fill your head, energizing you, sipping slowly to allow the taste to linger on your tongue. You drown out the noises at the kitchen table and ignore the bickering, the "Mommy," the cup of milk you hear overturn, and the argument over the prize in the cereal box. Who's turn is it? You can't even remember. Who cares anyway? You know you'll find it stuffed under the couch or somewhere on the kitchen floor the next day anyway, forgotten or broken.

For a few cherished moments, the kids join you and curl up beside you, gently kissing you and you laugh together at the TV. Maybe the morning can be saved, you decide. You cuddle and enjoy the time until suddenly someone notices that the kitten has just pooped on the floor so everyone has to go see. The phone rings, you reach for paper towels to clean up after the kitty and the sleeve to your bathrobe catches in the bowl of milk left from breakfast. Crash! There goes the bowl. Your sleeve is soaked, the girls begin doing cartwheels in the kitchen, and your son does the unspeakable. He approaches you with his first words of the day before you have even poured your precious and most desired second cup of coffee, "What are we going to do today?"

Your body freezes. You slowly sit your coffee cup down. You unconsciously bite your lip. You clench your jaws so tightly that your face hurts from the strain. Your eyes fixate on your children and you know that you have lost control as you hear yourself shout, "It's only 9:30. Tomorrow I'm getting a babysitter! I can't handle this!"

## EITHER KNOCK ME OUT OR COMMIT ME AND PLEASE HURRY!

You didn't realize when you gave birth to your second or third child that having more than three people in your family meant that it would be statistically impossible to have everyone happy at the same moment in time. Even with an "only" child you didn't realize you couldn't possibly be your child's playmate 18 hours a day. But you tried!

Having grown up watching families like "Donna Reed," the "Cleaver Family", "Father Knows Best," and the "Nelson Family," you thought you could do it all. Your family would be a picture book, TV type family. Perhaps you grew up in a very happy family. Perhaps you grew up in a family of screamers. Whatever your upbringing, you thought your family would be perfect.

Then, little by little, daily events crept in to shade your thinking.

"We need to go to your brother's ball game," you announce. "Fifteen more minutes to play, then we need to get ready." (Your parenting skills have taught you to always give a warning to help prepare for transitions.)

"But I don't wanna go," your younger one whines.

"I'm sorry," you reply, "but daddy is working late and I have to take you with me. Your brother has to be there in just a few minutes."

"But I don't wanna go! I want to stay here and play. Lisa and I were just starting to make up a game!" Your beautiful daughter throws herself onto the floor in a temper tantrum, refusing to get up, refusing to put on shoes, refusing to move while her screams grow louder.

You apologize, you coax, you bribe, you count, you put your foot down, and you listen to her complain and cry and moan. You carry her limp body to the car, ignoring the temper tantrum as best you can. While you silently feel a little sorry for her for disturbing her play you also feel a headache coming on. You may even offer to take the neighbor with you as a playmate (just what you want, one more child to watch out for at the ballpark). You survive the evening, but when your husband walks in the door, exhausted and stressed from his day, the two of you engage in a Mexican stand off for sympathy.

The next day you begin with a fresh attitude once again. It's Friday night, family night at your house. "Let's all go out to dinner," your husband suggests.

Great, you think. No dishes tonight.

"Where would everyone like to go?" (The $100 question.)

"McDonalds!"

"No, I want pizza."

"McDonalds!"

"Pizza!"

"Anywhere my friends won't be," your teenager mumbles, ducking his head down in the car so no one can see him.

Can't we agree on anything, you think.

"How about Chinese," Dad suggests.

"No, you know I don't like Chinese."

Your family fun night turns into a family battle and you become the referee.

Life becomes a series of daily struggles to keep the forces, personalities, ideas and wants of the individuals in your family separate, respected, and at times, to try to bring them to a compromising middle ground; a never ending challenge of parenting that seemed so simple on the TV families.

The next day: a new day, a new start you tell yourself. You once again awake, cleanse your breath and start with a fresh (but somewhat stilted) positive attitude.

Clouds gather in the sky smacking together in thunderous roars. Torrential rains set in for the day.

"How about a movie?" you offer unfolding the newspaper to search for the listings.

"Let's go see that new cartoon movie," your youngest begs.

"No, I want to see the action one."

"That won't be any good. I want to see the one about horses."

"But there's no words in that, just animals."

"I know, but I love animals."

"Well, I don't! You got to pick last time. I want to see the new love story."

You look up from the paper in dismay, "That's R rated," you interject.

"Well, Bobby's mom lets him see R rated movies. Everybody in my class has already seen it!"

You shake your head as you listen to them argue. The phone rings.

"Mom, can I spend the night with Becky?" "Please, please, please!"

One of your other children looks at you, "That's not fair. I won't have anyone to spend the night with." He stomps his feet, "It's not fair!"

"It's not fair!" You've heard that expression so many times. You remember using it on your parents. You don't remember quite when it was that you just accepted that life isn't fair but you remember fighting it painfully. You choke on the urge to lecture your children about the fairness of the world at this moment like your parents lectured you. Sometimes you may give in to this urge and cite examples of the real things in life that are truly unfair. But for now you resist. You close your eyes and let your meditation take you to a world beyond the arguing voices.

For a brief interlude, your mind floats into an out of body experience and you beg, "Either knock me out or commit me and please hurry!"

# DON'T DO IT ALONE:
# IT'S TRUE, THERE'S SAFETY IN NUMBERS!

"Battle stations everyone! Man your battle stations!" Combat boots on, salute, ready.

Some days you feel more like you're in combat than raising a family. Puppy dog eyes and angelic voices plead with you, "Please, please let us stay up late. We promise we'll be good tomorrow. Promise. We were good last time."

The puppy dog eyes always melt your resistance and the soft peck on the cheek clinches the deal. You topple off your battle station, knowing that you will suffer for your lack of strength in the morning.

The morning after arrives and yesterday's promises disappear as quickly as the snacks in your pantry. Your sentence to a day with tired children begins as you expected.

The telephone rings. The voice sounds vaguely familiar but you aren't sure. "How about a cup of coffee?" the voice says. It sounds like an adult. Amidst the goo-goo ga-ga's and the cooing of your infant, the shrilling screams and "mine" of your toddler, the "why's" of the pre schooler, the giggles and sassy back talk of the elementary age, the "What can we do today" of the adolescent, and the silence of the teenager, another adult voice spoke. It might be the voice of a friend, a neighbor, a mere acquaintance, but the adult voice on the other end sounds like music.

You feel starved for adult company some days. You stand in line at the grocery store trying to make friends with the lady behind you. You search through the department store for another mother with a stroller to talk to. You plant yourself next to a woman with three children at the local McDonald's and strike up a conversation.

The voice on the phone rings in your ear. You look around at the scattered toys, the dishes, the laundry piled in the corner. You don't have anything freshly baked to offer with coffee. Company might upset the baby's schedule. You stutter and mumble and almost decline. But something grabs your voice and thrusts out the words "Sure, come on over."

You hastily scramble around to clear a path and scrub the coffee pot to put on fresh coffee. A few doughnuts left from yesterday will do, just zap them in the microwave for a few seconds. A quick comb through your hair and brush on a little powder and you're set.

The coffee is fine and although you and your visitor rarely finish a complete sentence without an interruption from one of the children, you feel a friendship has deepened. You feel a renewal of your spirit. You feel like human again.

Although you adore being home with your children, sometimes you long for the conversation of an adult during the day. Talk shows, the radio, the newspaper, and TV help keep you informed and entertained, but the actual exchange of conversation, the interest of another person, and the sharing of ideas is needed.

After all, cows travel in herds, geese in flocks, fish in schools, birds migrate in groups, and like animals, people are definitely group oriented. Football players don't try to win the game without a team. Teachers have a lounge to congregate in and share stories of the day. The President even has a cabinet to help him. People are social beings and lately you have missed that social side of life.

You've lived and worked in groups since you were little. From preschool to elementary school, middle school and high school, then college, your job. Now you find yourself at home. With the same four walls to stare at all day, the limitations of conversation with children, the stimulation and motivation to maintain an interesting adult personality without other adults around poses a real challenge.

To your own horror, one day, you might even find yourself losing your temper with your child, being that parent you never wanted to be. You were up all night with your crying baby, an ear ache again. Your toddler crawled out of bed at 5:45 ready for the day. The toilet stopped up and over flowed. Your first grader put an M & M up her nose and you had to call the poison control center. You had to drive the car pool because the other mother is out of town. Your head starts to throb and before you can take some aspirin your strong willed child decides to test his limits as well as yours. He is adept at pushing all the right buttons and you begin to boil inside. As he watches your sparks ignite he steps over the line. He laughs. He seems to be taking some sweet pleasure in annoying you today. Your warnings, your strong voice, your demand for him to go to his room are ignored and seem comical to him. Then, for the first time in your life, you feel a rage inside. You clench your hands tightly. Your tongue is practicing unspeakable words and your thoughts are anything but maternal. You feel your voice escalating into a scream and, hopefully, You Leave the Room! You go into the bathroom, bedroom, garage, anywhere you can to escape your child and your own feelings. For the first time in your life, you feel out of control.

Do "good" parents feel this way? Do "good" parents ever feel out of control? Certainly, remember parents are people, too. What should you do when you have these feelings?

First, recognizing when you are reaching the point of losing control is the key. Once you recognize that moment, take action; not against your child, but for yourself. Take a few moments, minutes, whatever you need to calm yourself down. Make sure your child is in a safe place if he or she is an infant or toddler. If older, give them a brief message that you're on your own for a few minutes. Take the time!

Making sure that you have planned enough time for yourself each day and week can also help prevent these types of explosions. Also, if you need, call a friend. Hearing another person's voice on the phone can calm you, help you to verbalize your feelings, and prevent you from acting until you have calmed down. Having friends throughout parenting is a necessity. Sharing problems, daily stresses of parenting, an understanding nod from "someone who understands" is essential.

Remember when you were a child and you wanted to do something with your friends, for instance like go to a movie. You all huddled together to make a plan. You told your parents that the other kid's parents were letting them go. Then each of your friends told their parents the same story. If you came in late from a date, you always planned your story with your friends. You always asked for money or a privilege when a friend was over because you knew your folks wouldn't yell at you in front of others. Even as a kid your realized the importance of group combat. Wasn't that safety in numbers! Parents have to band together to support each other through the years, too.

Then parents are faced with that parental peer pressure. "Johnny's parents let him do whatever he wants." "Debbie's been dating since she was fourteen." "My friends all got mad because we had to leave early. You're the only parent that cared how late we stayed. Now they're all mad at me. They probably won't even invite me next time." This type of parental pressure begins early and you as a parent have to be ready with your approach. The fine line between "letting go" and being pulled along by your child and his or her demands to "keep up with the crowd" makes your wrinkles pop out.

What can you do? Man your battle stations, prepare for combat and don't do it alone. Remember, it's true, there's safety in numbers!

**TIPS**

- Make an effort to maintain one or two close friendships. A comforting word from a friend, an understanding "I'm in the same spot" can last forever.

- Plan regular outings with your children and without. Line up the babysitters.

- If you have recently moved, make an effort to join a group of some kind to help you meet people. Churches, clubs, neighborhood organizations, schools, community and city services are all ways to make friends. Like the commercial says, "Reach out and touch someone." Don't count on other people to find you. Take steps to make friends yourself. Don't be afraid to search out a new acquaintance. That person may need an understanding friend just as much as you.

- Support groups can be found formally or informally in many different places; church or church groups, local school parent programs and classes (you can learn something and make friends), neighborhood groups, clubs in the area such as art clubs, craft classes, play groups offered through schools, churches, neighborhoods, etc., exercise classes or health clubs.

- Don't forget about families. While sometimes they may add tension, they can be helpful babysitters. You and your mom or dad might just become friends one day while you sit and talk about life and the raising of children.

- Have visits and outings with your child and his/her friends that include parents.

- Get involved in your child's school or preschool. Get to know the teachers and other parents.

- If a play group isn't available in your neighborhood, start one yourself. Also join or start a babysitting co-op.

- Try to get to know the parents of your children's friends, even teenagers' parents. Talking and planning with these parents as well as the one's in your neighborhood helps you learn what their views are, enables you to understand and deal with peer pressure of children and their parents, and may help you all to form agreements on certain issues that might arise with your children.

- Establish your principles and values with your children and let them know your boundaries. Explain your reasons and set up consequences for actions that stay within boundaries and for actions that do not stay within boundaries. Children want and need boundaries to assure them that you care. Make your rules, be firm, consistent, as fair as possible, and if you make a mistake, discuss that, too. The role model you provide (how you react in situations) teaches them far more than your lectures and words. So in the face of peer pressure, (parental peer pressure) you and your child both know your views in advance. Listen, be understanding, flexible when you can, and learn to say "No" in a calm voice.

- Share your gripes, let off some steam, vent your frustrations about your children to your friends but do remember not to do it at your child's expense. Your child's self respect is fragile and can be damaged if they think you are telling your friends all their blunders and atrocities. Man your battle stations, wear your combat boots and helmet, but remember you still have to wear "kid gloves."

# CHAPTER 2

## LET'S BE REALISTIC:
## FIND YOUR HEAD AND
## SNAP IT ON FAST!

"A picture tells a thousand words." That's the old saying. That may be true but does the picture tell the real story. You thumb through your family photo album early one summer morning as you sip your coffee. Your eyes rest on the Easter picture you had taken in the spring. The cross made of flowers in front of your church made a perfect setting for your family photo. You remember laughing at your son's resistance to having his picture made, taking turns with the other families who shared your idea. Everyone smiled at the camera, so adorned in their new Easter clothes, hats, lace socks, and suits.

Looking at the photograph sends your mind on a nostalgic journey back in time to that day. You relive that Easter in your mind.

"Mommy, tie my bow." You touch the delicate lace on the collar of your daughter's dress, admiring its intricacy. Then you run your fingers down the satin sash and tie it into a perfect bow. Your pearl barrettes clasped in her hair are just the finishing touch and she looks like a magazine model. Your son emerges wearing his new suit and shiny new Sunday shoes, so handsome. He looks just like his father. A picturesque family, everyone set in their new Easter attire. You climb into your van and start for church. The warmth of sunshine can't exceed the warmth in your heart for the spring season, the special Easter service you always look forward to, the day planned with all your family members included.

"What time is the egg hunt, Mommy?" your youngest one asks.

"Everyone is suppose to come around 2:00," you answer.

"I can't wait," your children chant. You feel their excitement, thinking of the traditional family egg hunt, the past shared family occasions, the huge meal you know awaits, the scavenger hunt you secretly planned and the surprise prizes you chose.

You enter the church aglow with the beauty of your family. You sit side by side on the back pew. You feel so proud you know you must be radiating. The music begins and your little darlings begin also.

"Hand me that pencil."

"How long do we have to sit here?"

"Shh." you whisper.

Your son pokes your daughter in the side. She cries. "I want that pencil. It's darker." She grabs the pencil from her sister's hand and the offering cards from the back of the pew and begins scribbling on them.

"Give that back. I had it first." Your other daughter grabs for the pencil and accidently scribbles a pencil mark on her new dress as she pulls it away from her sister.

Your youngest taps her patent leather shoes against the back of the pew making tap dance sounds and you look at your son and see his lips protrude. Then he begins to roll his head around and around to entertain himself.

You stiffen, trying to motion for them to be quiet. You try to ignore them and the looks you know you are getting from the people behind you. The sermon gets lost in your thoughts as you strain to maintain control and a Christian attitude. Your family, the picture perfect family sat down together in church today. The photograph you have on the living room wall with everyone smiling is just like the one you carry in your wallet. Is it just that, a picture?

Yes, it is, a posed picture. Pretty clothes, beautiful music, and even church can't transform you into the perfect family.

Your tension subsides as you arrive home and everyone quickly changes for the day. The relatives arrive. The kids play in the yard, following your strict orders. You give a silent thanks for the cooperation of the weather today. Snacks and drinks are on the patio table. The hub bub of your extended family is a joy, only a few times a year do you all get to see each other.

It's time for the egg hunt, you decide as you see a few dark clouds appear above you. The kids retreat to the basement while the adults hide the eggs.

"Why do the little kids get to go first?" the big kids complain.

"These are too easy," one moans.

"I didn't find hardly any."

"She gots more than me."

You try to smooth everyone's feelings and have, afterall, thought enough in advance to have prepared and bought prizes for everyone.

Next the scavenger hunt; a big success, even though the adults groaned when they first learned they had to participate. Water guns are a delightful surprise for all the kids and the water battle begins.

Dinner is ready so a quick change to dry clothes is made for the kids. The adults file into the dining room. The children gather in the kitchen. Mounds of delicious foods are piled onto plates and everyone chooses his or her favorites.

As the adults finally sit down to dinner, wails of laughter, squeals, rude noises, and a food fight filter in from the kitchen. Why is it that the children are always so loud and rude at the table? You can't seem to understand this repeated phenomenon.

You try to finish dinner, the adults taking turns to remind the children of their manners. Coffee, dessert, late night good-byes and thanks for a wonderful day from the family members as they head for home. Exhausted, you face the dirty kitchen, the mounds of dishes and leftovers, the kids needing a bath, and the clock. 10:00. You try to hurry the kids to bed for tomorrow, you realize, is only a few short hours away.

"But you promised us a bubble bath tonight," one of your children cries.

"Darling, it's too late," you explain. "It's already way past your bedtime. Maybe tomorrow."

"But you promised tonight." Screeching cries pierce your ears and your fatigue borders on anger.

No, "Thanks, Mommy." No, "We had fun today, Mommy." No, "Thanks for letting us have an egg hunt." No, "Thanks for the new dress, Mom." The kids are just exhausted, you try to tell yourself. Ignore them. They're just kids and they're overtired. You kiss the kids goodnight, flip off the light, but feel a little sadness creep in as you head for the long job waiting on you in the kitchen.

You collapse into bed and the few hours you sleep seem like only minutes when you hear your children race down the stairs the next morning.

Those same footsteps bring you quickly back from your nostalgic trip in time. "I'm hungry."

"What's for breakfast?"

As soon as you pour cereal into the bowls the demands begin. "Mom, I need to be at practice at 3:30 today."

"Mom, you said Brittany could come over at 3:00 today."

"Well, I have to go to a birthday party at 2:45. We still have to go get a present, Mom."

"Mom, why isn't my uniform clean? I put it in the dirty clothes yesterday."

"Mom, you promised you'd take me shopping today. I have to have new cleats for baseball and I have to have them today."

You glance at the family photo in your lap, the picturesque family. Your head seems to be spinning in twenty directions. You don't feel like the picture perfect mom anymore but more like a juggler with too many balls and not enough hands. The dreamy eyes you woke with this morning see nothing but chaos all around.

"Mom, I'm ready. Hurry, I'm gonna be late. The coach will yell at me."

"Mom, when will you be back?"

"Mom, can you sew this hole up?"

Your head bounces in circles. You can't find your purse. You can't find your car keys. You can't find the garage door opener. You can't find your umbrella. But let's be realistic. Hurry, find your head, and snap it on fast!

# KIDS REALLY ARE PEOPLE

It is a proven fact. Kids really are people. Medical doctors have researched this question extensively. Psychiatrists and teachers have confirmed the studies, although teachers and parents seem reluctant to agree 100% at times.

Even though as parents you were mesmerized from the moment the doctor laid the miracle of birth in your arms, and instantly the maternal instinct you had wondered about during those last few months of swollen ankles, contractions and indigestion, overwhelmed every ounce of your being, as time passed hints of doubt began creeping in. Pregnancy and the joy and pain of childbirth became like war stories at women's gatherings and fatigue set in shortly after you arrived home. However, the vision of proudly carrying the most beautiful child ever born out of the hospital that day, the flowers, cards, balloons, visitors staring and raving over your newborn, and the special bond you formed the first moment your eyes saw your infant's face, the first time you touched the tiny helpless fingers, the first time your baby ever smiled would be among the first of the most treasured memories in your life. The meaning of small pleasures and wonders became gigantic and the powerful love that swelled within you was stronger than you could ever have imagined.

This tiny little body, so helpless, so precious, belonged to you. In your arms lay the little person who you would love, care for, guide, and mold into another human. A scary thought, so scary that for the first time you understood some of the lectures your own mother had given you about how she loved you more than life itself, how she sacrificed for you, and how those spankings she gave you hurt her more than they hurt you.

Euphoria lasted until post partum began, which, even if you had read about it, you still weren't prepared for the unexplained emotions you felt. Tears of joy and sadness pooled together. Happiness and fear were all wrapped up in that little bundle. The lingering baby fat and weeks of sleepless nights stretched into fatigue and forced you to wonder if your life would ever be back to normal. And would it?

Probably not! Your child rearing stage had begun and there was no turning back. Not that you would want to, you reminded yourself as you gazed at the most precious of all our gifts; the gift of life. But nonetheless, there were adjustments to be made. Suddenly your time was very limited. Your neat house became disorderly. You and your husband may have fought over who's turn it was to get up with the baby or to babysit. Your first experiences with waiting in the pediatrician's office, a crying baby in a restaurant, not fitting into your clothes (or worse yet, a stranger asking you when your baby was due, three months after you gave birth), and the problem of finding time to get a shower, dress, and perhaps splash on a little makeup before lunchtime were unexpected realizations.

As time passed, your infant grew and miraculously changed into a crawler, a toddler, then a child. Yes, a little person. Of course, in your B.C. years, you had envisioned hours of sweet blissful play with your child.

You do have moments like that. You also have had hours of chasing an active toddler, rescuing him from electrical sockets, open toilets and ledges. You thought your child would always love you and listen to whatever you said. Never would your child throw a temper tantrum in a public place or hide under the clothes in the store or do any other embarrassing thing (unspeakables) in public. Upon witnessing a stranger's child misbehaving in public, you might have even announced to a friend, "No child of mine would ever do that!"

Then one day it happened. You were standing in line to check out at the grocery store and your child began to beg for candy. In your sweet patient voice you said, "No, darling, we're going to eat dinner when we get home. I'm fixing chicken and potatoes, your favorites."

To your amazement, your child suddenly bellowed out, "No, I want candy. You know I hate chicken. Yuk! Why do you always make me eat those awful things? You're so mean!"

As you tried then to reason with your child, write your check and maintain a smile while the entire store watched, your child then tossed the egg carton on the floor sending cracked eggs all over the grocery cart and your foot, grabbed a pack of bubble gum and ran for the door. You stood there in complete and utter awe. This precious little angel that you adore and would give your life for just crossed the line. You darted after him just to keep him from running in front of the cars in the parking lot and you fought the unpleasant urges you felt inside. Then after you retrieved the seven bags of groceries you had left sitting inside the store, tried to hold your head up high and ignore the people staring, you finally forced him into the car, loaded the groceries, and slid behind the wheel. Then you heard him mutter, "Sam's mom is nicer than you. She always lets him get candy and she lets him eat whatever he wants." Your hands gripped the steering wheel so hard they ached. You bit your lip and fire seeped from the corner of your mouth as a tear rolled down your cheek.

How could this child that you adore, this child that you have loved, nurtured and rocked to sleep at night speak to you like this!

Don't worry, your reaction is normal and somewhat justified. Afterall, Parents Are People, Too. (See the next section.)

Your child is only acting like a child and as difficult as it may be, one of your first lessons as a parent is not to take it personally. Children are individuals from the moment they are born. No two may react exactly the same. However, there are certain characteristics that seem common at different ages. Make yourself aware of these so you know what to expect. Remember a child is a child, not a small adult. He has feelings, opinions, and his own set of reactions which are influenced by his age. He doesn't see the world as you do, doesn't have the maturity of the adult, although adults often have the maturity of their children.

The following is a famous poem that has been quoted. You may want to copy this and hang it on your refrigerator for reference when you are having a doubtful moment.

## A CHILD IS A PERSON

*A child is not a possession or an object to be shaped by adults as they desire.*

*A child is a Person, an immortal soul living in a physical body, trusted for a while to the care and guidance of parents or parent substitutes.*

*Treat every child as a Person. Treat him as you yourself like to be treated.*

*Be courteous to him.*

*Consider his feelings.*

*Do not insult him.*

*Do not belittle or make fun of him.*

*Do not intentionally embarrass him.*

*Trust him, and let him know that you do.*

*If you wish a child to respect you, you must earn his respect.*

*Show respect for him as a Person, an individual being of value and importance.*

*A child learns by imitation. When you are considerate and kind, trustworthy and honest, courteous and respectful, you teach him to be likewise.*

*Above all, love him consistently and unselfishly.*

--AUTHOR UNKNOWN

The following is a list of characteristics common for different age levels. Some paraphrasing of characteristics was taken from books written by Dr. Arnold Gesell. The titles appear in the section "Additional Resources." Other books may give more detailed descriptions. This is a general overview to help you, as a parent, know what to expect and to help you better cope. Most importantly, all children need to be loved unconditionally, regardless of their actions. When disciplining your child, be sure to emphasize approval or disapproval of actions and specific behaviors, not the child personally. A good self concept is the best gift you can give your child.

### CHARACTERISTICS OF CHILDREN BY AGE

**INFANT**: communicates needs by laughing, crying, very physical, needs should be met for physical and emotional security to be established, may become attached to mom, needs love and nurturing

**ONE-TWO**: physical development advances rapidly, explores environment with hands, feet, etc. Responds to love, affection, likes games like pat-a-cake and peek-a-boo, begins walking and running, 18 months to two begins developing some independence, "I can do it myself," stubborn, may want to dress self, etc., temper tantrums may occur out of frustration and need to establish independence (commonly known as the terrible two's), language develops, favorite words are "no" and "mine," likes to do opposite of what you tell him.

**THREE:** "trusting threes," sharing, happy, friendly, conforming, at three there is good motor control, but 3 1/2 may be insecure physically, loves reading, three dresses self, 3 1/2 may use daily routine to battle and control his mom.

**FOUR:** "wild and wonderful," behavior seems out of bounds, laughs and cries loudly, can copy simple shapes, may be interested in puzzles, cutting, gross motor activities, likes to be silly, sentence structure improving, questions everything, "Why?"

**FIVE:** imaginative, egocentrical, friendly, can organize games, plays in group, loves parents and teachers, cooperative but stubborn, active and noisy, learns best with "hands on" type activities, wants to be "big," likes to learn, interested in words, may have bad dreams.

**SIX:** mother not center of universe anymore, he is the center of his own world, wants to be first, to be loved the best, to have the most of everything, demanding, may defy and dawdle, enthusiastic but demanding, likes school type work, mealtime chaotic, loves mother but when things go wrong may take it out on her.

**SEVEN:** begins to socialize more, parents not the center as much as friends, begins to eat with friends more, observes differences in families, generally cooperative.

**EIGHT:** asserts independence more, "Mother" becomes used, enjoys reading, especially likes silly jokes, can be helpful at home when coaxed properly, graduates to bigger bike, begins demanding a little independence in the neighborhood.

**NINE:** seems to be outgrowing toys, outside activities important, still likes school but may become frustrated with homework.

**TEN:** age of equilibrium, good adjustment, comfortable, nice person, loves his family, gets along with peers, likes collections, may want privacy, may have difficulty falling asleep, reduces time of sleeping, room is a mess, least tearful age, respects teachers.

**ELEVEN:** the opposite of ten, time of breaking up, discord, trial and error in testing limits, perpetual chip on shoulder, behaves like a beginning adolescent, egocentric and energetic, constantly on the go eating and talking, critical of mother, not helpful around house, work hard for grades, mood changes, fat period due to physical changes, fights going to bed, heavy and hard sleepers and hard to get up in a.m., may be embarrassed by parents in public, likes school, may cheat in games, most tearful age.

**TWELVE:** calm, comfortable and secure with themselves, friendly, objectively detached from mom, physically mature, sexually for some, some interest in boy-girl relationships, siblings still fight, boys like sports, girls interested in caring for young children, bouts of fatigue or sharp pains in head or abdomen, feet, etc., due to onset of puberty, don't fight bedtime as much but are lighter sleepers, like to fix up own room, biggest worry is schoolwork, good sense of humor, likes dirty jokes, both sex parties, conscience is demanding.

**THIRTEEN:** quiet, inwardizing, withdrawn, uncommunicative, think about things, withdrawn from family, keeps door closed and locked, worries about body and self, complains that people don't understand him, not sociable with adults, need lots of money but not responsible with it, sensitive, snaps at parents, feels persecuted when parents criticize, may be annoyed with siblings, friendships important, not as childish.

**FOURTEEN:** time of vigor, energy and excitement, school is okay, extracurricular activities fill day with fun and pleasure, may begin to criticize father, walks at least five feet away from parents in store, still searching for self and identity, still loves parents but rarely shows it, parents are embarrassing, likes parties, 14 to 15 boys cross line from looking like a boy to a man, parents need support groups, show more care for room and clothes, likes sports and social gatherings

**FIFTEEN:** wants independence, thinks everything adult does is wrong, wants to be free of family, gets along better with siblings, dating is pleasurable and painful, show interest in intellectual plans for future, parents need to try and respect need for independence, easier to get children to comment or talk if parent shows lack of desire.

**SIXTEEN:** "sweet sixteen," smooth and comfortable age, friendly and more cooperative to family, more poised and self-sufficient, loves friends and parties

Becoming familiar with these characteristics doesn't always mean it is easy to cope, but keeping them in mind and knowing that they are common among other children should comfort you. Try to be loving but objective when you're dealing with problems that arise, keeping in mind that, although hard to believe at times, kids really are people. It's almost impossible sometimes, but remind yourself that you are doing the best you can. Don't be too hard on yourself. After all, it's true; PARENTS ARE PEOPLE, TOO.

# THE SHOCKING TRUTH:
# PARENTS ARE PEOPLE TOO!

So you decided to have kids of your own. It sounded so romantic in the beginning. When the movie and televisions stars looked dreamily at their wives or lovers and said, "She's having my baby," cold chills ran up your spine. With a tear in the corner of his eye he touched her blossoming stomach and tenderly looked into her eyes and said, "You've never looked more beautiful and more passionate than you do at this moment." You wanted to sob. What is more special, more tender, and more romantic? What else could bring two people closer together than the making, giving birth and raising of a child?

As soon as your toes disappeared underneath the watermelon in front of you everything changed. Your ankles turned to cantaloupes. Your sleep patterns were disturbed. You forced pillows under parts of your body you didn't know existed just to get comfortable. Your sex life became an art of mastering strange positions and a little of the romance sifted out of the bowl. He never quite looked at you with those dreamy eyes and said, "She's having my baby." At least not the way you pictured. And your husband, he was thrust onto the roller coaster of women's hormones and wasn't quite sure whether to jump off or hang on. No matter how hard he tried or what he did, there were times when it just wasn't right. You weren't sure what was going on and neither was he. However, childbirth and those first glorious moments of seeing that infant jogged your memory and you were on your way to parenting, not yet aware though of the changes that would slowly overtake your life.

"Not me, I'm not changing the way I live," you had declared. "I'm not going to be one of those people who just talk about their kids all the time. You'll never hear me talking about the red crayons my child ate and how it made his poop turn red. NOT ME!"

But the way grapes turn to raisins, one day you did. You may have suddenly realized the transformation that took place or perhaps a friend reminded you one day as you called and spent thirty minutes describing how you made your own baby food or how proud you were of your teenager for working at the local hamburger spot.

The absorption with your family continued to grow until one day you forgot your own name and your child looked at you and said, "That's what Mommy's are for, to clean up and fix us food." Without understanding why, you suddenly burst into tears and screamed, "Mommy's are people, too!"

## TAKE THE TEST:

If any of the statements below sound familiar you are well into the parenting stage and admit doubts of your own that you truly are a person.

*You Know You're a Mother And Aren't Sure if You're Really A Person When:*

- A child says, "Mommy" and you automatically turn and answer (even if your kids aren't with you).

- You now sympathize with other mothers when their child has a temper tantrum in public.

- When you see a father alone with his kids, having a difficult time, you either laugh or jump in to help.

- When the phone rings, you yell, "You might as well answer it, you know it's for you. No one ever calls me anymore."

- When you go out to eat without children, you request to move if you are seated next to a family with kids.

- You cut your husband's meat or if you're sharing a dessert with a friend, you make sure the pieces are exactly even.

- You always carry baby wipes in your car.

- When you are alone in your car, you find yourself listening to "Wee Sing" tapes.

- When you sit watching your child's ballgame or recital, other children seem to be drawn to you, sit beside you and talk to you the entire time. You always seem to have a car full of extra children with you and your yard is covered with children and an assortment of big wheels, roller skates, bikes, and balls at all times.

- Someone at the pool asks you if you know how to swim, since they've only seen you standing in the shallow end with kids hanging all over you.

- You correct other children in your neighborhood and at the grocery store.

- You never close the bathroom door so you can hear if a disaster occurs.

- You wake frantically throwing the covers off you, thinking you fell asleep with your newborn in your arms and forgot to put him back in his crib.

- You constantly dream you forgot one of your children.

- You forget one of your children.

- You find yourself smirking and say, "I can't wait until you have children of your own."

- You cry because your child is sad. You're depressed and worry because he or she didn't make the team or doesn't have a boyfriend.

- You want to call your child's teacher and tell her how tired you are of homework, but he begs you not to.

- You yell at a coach, "Why don't you let my child play?"

*You Know You're A Daddy and Aren't Sure if You Are a Person When:*

- You trip over skates, bats, balls, big wheels and other toys as you get out of the car.

- When you drive into your driveway it looks like a bicycle junkyard.

- You stay up all night Christmas eve putting toys together.

- Everyone in the entire family thinks you always know how to "fix it."

- You agree to coach little league and try to fit that into your busy schedule.

- You insist your kids eat eggs for breakfast even though you hated eating them when you were a kid.

- You rise at 5:00 a.m. just to have a few minutes peace to read the paper.

- You remind your wife to call you if she's going to be out after 10:00.

- You tell your wife if she shows she can be responsible with the money, you'll buy her a new car.

- You can fall asleep with three children sitting on your head.

- You look at your child and say, "Those are my M & M's, and I'm not sharing."

- You keep an extra tie in your car to change into after you wear the one your son or daughter gave you for Christmas.

- You don't play golf so you can save money for the new tennis shoes your child wants.

OKAY, YOU PASSED THE TEST! You may be in doubt at times that you are truly a person, but if you must, perform hypnosis on yourself and try to remember that fact. You live, you breathe, you'd die for your kids. Or should you? Well, die for them, most probably, but live and breathe, not completely. It takes constant effort to remember your own needs, but remember them you must. Then the challenge begins; trying to juggle their needs, your needs, the time for them, the time for you, the time for your spouse. Perhaps one day someone will invent a time machine to help parents schedule their lives with their children. Surely it will sell for $19.95 on TV, and I'll dial the 800 number immediately and place my order.

# SUPER MOMS:
# NO SUCH THING!

Calling all super moms! Calling all super moms! Did anyone answer? If you did, I hope you're writing your own book so the rest of us can learn how to achieve the unachievable.

The pressure to be this super mom, to do it all! The washing machine is overloaded, the soap oozes out, the spin cycle accele-ates, the door pops open and out spills the sudsy waters. Is that really our washing machine or our lives?

Women are thankful of the advantages modern views and women's libbers have given us, but with them also have come an array of problems, choices, and a confusion of roles for both parents. Do I work? Do I stay home? What about childcare? I must work! We need the money. Enough! Let's face it, no easy solution exists. Every family has to assess its own situation and adapt accordingly. Numerous articles and boundless research exist discussing the "super mom" phenomenon. Most tend to view it as a product of the changing roles and views in our society as well as economic influ-ences that dictate our lives. However, some men and women have difficulty coping with the decisions and the adjustments being made.

In prior years, women were expected to be sole child caretakers. The choices today provide opportunities for women to pursue successful careers or to stay home by choice. Some feel they have no choice but to work, due to financial reasons. Whatever the decision, women are often plagued with the big "G"–guilt. Guilt for not staying home with the children, anxiety over childcare, and trying to do it all or staying home and sacrificing the fulfillment of a career and monetary rewards creates conflict. Self-esteem may plunge in some instances, especially if the woman doesn't have a good support group. Often women making the choice of staying home feel unappreciated and feel they don't get the respect of others. When asked "what do you do?" the answer, "I stay home with my children" is often followed by sighs of "Oh, you don't do anything." Either group of women often envies the other.

So, I offer no answer but to accept that super moms—No Such Thing!

Take your head out of the clouds and remember Parents Are People, Too! (At least we were before children.)

Accept your choice and your children will also. A happier mom, no matter what her choice, raises happier children. Be kind to yourself and just do the best you can; what better model can you be for your kids.

Remember your cartoon days: "Uh, Uh, That's Life, Folks!"

## THE MIDLIFE CRISIS

While your baby naps blissfully in the other room, you knead the bread dough, rolling it between your hands, pressing and feeling its warmth. Your favorite tape is playing in the background and you hum along thinking about how nice it is to be here in the warmth of your home instead of battling the rush hour traffic and the hassles of a job outside the home. A fresh pot of coffee is brewing and your neighbor drops over for a chat. You sit and sip coffee, sharing some homemade cinnamon rolls you made just this morning. You trade childbirth stories like war veterans trade war stories and show off your stretch marks, stroking them tenderly as a wine connoisseur strokes the rim of his glass before tasting. Shockingly content with your days at home with your children you are eager for the school bus to arrive and summer to begin. You listen for the roar of the bus and greet your kids at the door, hot brownies and cold milk in your hand. Your children's chatter telling about their day is like a sweet melody to your ears. A stage of your life you've dreamed of, anticipated, or if you are a working mother, perhaps feel like you are missing.

Your days may go on forever like this (after all you do believe in miracles, Santa Claus, fairies and Peter Pan) or one day, either due to extreme PMS, burnout, or a mid-life crisis, you may find yourself struggling to climb into your van. Your body fights itself to run, to escape the rut you seem to have fallen into. Is your life no more than running a taxi service? Is life no more than cleaning up spills, trash and the toys that seem to reappear from nowhere? Is life no more than washing, folding, refolding, mopping, cooking, packing lunches and daily trips to the supermarket because, as your children have so kindly reminded you, "Mom, there's nothing good to eat in the house!" Can you survive the summer with kids and a midlife crisis?

Your mother spends the night with you one night and as you sit down with a glass of wine in hand after getting the children to bed, she reminds you, "Now, honey, that could get to be a habit one day."

You twist your jaws and close your eyes momentarily to soften the urge you feel inside. "Mother," you reply looking up at her, "it's the only adult thing I do!"

### Possible Events that May Trigger or Lead to A Mid-life Crisis

You eye a tiny red convertible racing along the highway. An attractive brunette whose hair is catching in the wind and wisping across her face strokes the wheel. Her lips move with the music and she seems to know exactly where she is going or either she doesn't and she doesn't care. She's just there for the ride.

You go to a dinner party with your husband and find yourself standing idly. You wonder if anyone else saw Donahue or your favorite soap. You start to tell about the great movie you saw the other night. Then you remember, it was a Disney. One of the young executive women speaks politely to you, touches the collar of your silk blouse, and says, "Gee, I didn't know Mothers had clothes like this." You stare at her blankly, bite your lip and tongue and reply, "Yeah, we clean up pretty good."

Your twelve year old daughter walks into the room. "Mom, this is too little for me. Do you want it?" Your eyes look up to find her holding one of her bras.

You have to pick up your child from school and she sees you, avoids you completely and walks around the school to get to your car. Then she asks you next time to not pull up "right in front of the school and not to bring the van."

Your child graduates from anything; diapers, thumb sucking, kindergarten, middle school, high school, etc.

You give your child a pep talk one day , "Don't give up, if you don't do well at first, just try, try again. That's what I do. I really admire and am proud of you for trying." Your child looks at you and says, "Well, Mom, but you never try anything new."

You sip on a glass of wine one evening and your child looks at you and says, "Mom, you know that's a drug. Why don't you want me to drink it if you do?" A TOUGH CALL! You find yourself very confused. You want to be honest with your children. You are behind the anti-drug programs, yet you are an adult, a responsible adult. You don't drink and drive. You don't get sloshed. You just enjoy an occasional drink. You fumble with your words. You try to talk to your child and pray he'll understand and see the difference. Then you try to understand yourself.

You start to tie your daughter's long t-shirt into a knot at the waist. She stops you and stays, "Mom, that's not the style in third grade now, even the teachers know that."

Your mother stops by for a visit and while she inspects the refrigerator to see if you've cleaned it lately she comments, "Honey, you know you have more gray hair than I do."

You complain to your OBGYN that you are having migrains. He smirks and says, "Well, you know I hate to tell you this, but you are getting a little older, dear."

You try on your bathing suit for the summer and discover what "the cottage cheese look" means: cellulite!

You are in the store looking at the latest fashions. You pick up a fancy jean jacket (for yourself) and the young clerk asks you what size your daughter wears. She then tries it on to show you how cute it is.

The bag boys in the grocery store call you Ma'am.

The sign at the liquor store says they card everyone, but you don't get carded.

Your toddler laughingly points to your face and says, "Mama, what are those pretty lines on your face?"

You go shopping for a new bathing suit, a chore as bad as cleaning. You search the racks but discover that there is no bathing suit that covers varicose veins.

You are bathing suit shopping with your daughter and she points to a hanger, "Here, Mom, how about this one." You look and see the skirt attached to the bottom.

You start to take a walk with a friend on the beach and your husband whispers in your ear, "Honey, why don't you put on a shirt over your bathing suit. You don't want to embarrass yourself."

You see relatives at the family reunion and they constantly remind you that you look more and more like your mother every day.

Famous old songs keep ringing in your mind like "Nobody told me they'd be days like this," "On the Road Again," and "We Got to Get Out Of This Place."

OKAY, you are full fledge in your mid-life crisis. You realize it. You admit it. And you don't want to analyze it. You've thought of twenty different jobs you'd like to try. You highlight your hair. You buy the short skirt. Then you give in and buy the convertible. After all, you were from a meager background and you and your husband have worked hard for years. You've sacrificed for the kids. You can afford it. Your head is floating as you drive home. The stereo is blasting and you don't care if you will look silly in February with the top down. That night, you put the kids to bed and you and your husband sneak out to sit in it for a few minutes, a glass of wine and soft music (you're still in the garage), because even though you are having a mid-life crisis you still are responsible and won't leave the kids alone at night. You make a toast and just as you do your 11-year-old opens the door, shakes his head and mutters, "Ya'll are crazy." You and your husband chuckle. The child thinks his parents have lost their minds. Then he says, "And, by the way, could you just keep the music down a little." You laugh, thinking "isn't something wrong with this picture." Then you turn the music up as Rod Stewart sings, "Forever Young." The rest, like they say, is up to your imagination.

---

# DADS: THE OTHER SIDE OF THE COIN

The coin spins and twists and turns in the air and begins its descent towards the floor. Heads or tails; mom or dad? Which way will it land? There are two sides to every coin. For every joy and frustration mom experiences, Dad has his own.

The coin just landed with Dad face up. You're finally calling it a day at the office, job, trucking company, whatever your place of employment. You toss the briefcase or hardhat in the back seat, place the key in the ignition, and settle in for the daily traffic battle home. Your collar sticks to your neck in the heat and the jacket and tie shed themselves while you crank up the air conditioner. "95 degrees" you hear the disk jockey say. It feels more like 200. Your mind is still boggled with meetings, business deals on the verge of ruin, decisions to be made, the building unfinished, the job undone. The car phone rings and your ears meet with more problems that can't seem to wait. You try to calm the investor, the secretary and the boss while you weave your way through rush hour traffic, red lights and bumper fenders.

You finally rectify another daily crisis, at least for the moment, and after three nights of business dinners or overtime, you begin to anticipate a good home cooked meal and a quiet night with the family. Your ride home isn't long enough to completely rid you of tension or is so long that it only adds to your tensions and you haven't completely switched gears from breadwinner to "Father Knows Best" when you steer your car into the driveway.

Your yard looks like a toy store and you can't pull into the garage because of the scattered bicycles and toys that have taken over your parking space. One of your children waves to you and you wave back, but who are all those other kids in your yard? You recognize a couple of them, but where did the teenager with the punk hairdo come from, and who is that boy holding your daughter's hand and standing close to her.

You play dodge ball with the skates, bats, balls and riding toys in the garage but manage to take it in your stride, knowing that behind that door is a loving family waiting for you with open arms, looking forward to seeing you, and thankful for all your hard work.

As you turn the doorknob, the familiar squeak of the door sounds like music. But just as you open the door, you hear a shriek. Next comes your wife's voice in anything but a pleasant tone.

"Listen here, young man, you don't need to talk to me that way!"

"I'll do what I want!" he screams.

Your child marches through the kitchen, quickly passes you without a word, and slams the door. Your wife tosses her hands in the air, muttering unspeakables under her breath, and you realize you have walked in right in the middle of the arsenic hour.

"What was that all about?" you ask. Then without thinking, you begin automatically searching the kitchen for that home cooked dinner and you ask, "What's for dinner?"

Your wife sends you an unfriendly glare and huffs away, mumbling, "Hot dogs." You immediately assess the situation. She's either had a bad day or you mentally note the day on the calendar to see if it's that time of the month again. You follow her and give her a gentle kiss, "Honey, what's wrong. Did you have a bad day?"

Well, you asked for it. She is like a volcano waiting to erupt. One sentence leads to another and for the next thirty minutes you are loaded with the trivial upsets of her day, problems with the children, the broken washing machine, the orthodontist bill, the lecture about calling when you're going to be late, the description of how your son cried himself to sleep the night before because you missed his ball game, and the baby.

"Here," she says as she thrusts him into your arms. "I'm late. I'm supposed to be at the church for a meeting in 10 minutes." A quick peck on the cheek and she's out the door.

You sprawl on the floor to relax with the baby for a few minutes and can't help but notice the trail of toys, books, and clothes lining the floor. Your son walks in. The pitiful eyes that tell you of the game you missed the night before match the sour expression on his face. "Dad, will you throw the ball with me?"

"Not now, son, maybe in a few minutes."

"But, Dad, you said you'd help me learn to pitch and you haven't."

"After supper, I have to watch your little sister now."

"Dad! You promised."

His woe begotten face pinches your guilt button and you drag yourself up from the floor, the baby on your hip, and follow him outside. You get the baby settled in her walker with some toys and warm up your arm. Your son misses your first few pitches, screams that your aren't throwing them to him, and finally stomps off to sulk.

"Daddy, play with me," your other child whines, tugging at your shirt. You throw her around and chase her, falling into the thick grass. Need to cut the grass, you make a mental note.

"Daddy, I need new shoes for our program at church," one of your children says.

"Well, I need new shoes, too," your other child adds.

You trudge into the kitchen for the hotdogs and thumb through the mail on the counter while everyone washes hands. Bills, bills, and more bills.

Hotdogs are a treat for the kids and while you gobble yours down, your daughter complains about the vegetables and roast they had to eat the night before.

You and the kids watch a little TV after dinner, you manage to get the kids in the bathtub and pajamas on at a reasonable time. So, what, there's a little water on the floor and the wet towels are in a heap. At least you got them bathed. You're romping on the floor when your wife walks in. You can't help but notice how tan she looks. The days at the pool must be great. Then you notice the heavy sigh she breathes as she spots the dishes in the sink.

"I haven't had time," you apologize.

"Just take the little ones to bed," she orders, opening the dishwasher and piling the dishes in.

After much stalling and kicking you finally tuck the kids in bed, then join your wife in the kitchen to help her clean up.

"How was your meeting?" you ask.

"Okay," she answers. "But I'm worried about Sandra (the teenage daughter). She seems depressed lately. Every time I try to talk to her she just says, "Leave me alone, Mom. I just need to find myself.""

"I'll try to talk to her," you say, trying to comfort your wife. Then you sit down to face the monthly paying of the bills, trying to juggle the necessities, the wants, and the have to's and the can waits to make it all fit into your budget.

Stress, pressure, problems—you feel like you have to hold it all together. The weight of your family's survival financially rests on your shoulders or the guilt of needing your wife to work (those old fashioned standards are hard to erase), the pressure of "success" in your business, the demands of children and the roles of wife and husband which are to be negotiated on a daily basis, expectations as a husband and father, then time for yourself (where does that fit in). Dad, the coin may have landed with your side up, but sometimes it feels like your face is always down.

### TIPS

Reminder: Every coin has two sides. For all types of families, working mothers, single parents, traditional, at home fathers, and any of the combinations available, the grass may always look greener on the other side. However, if you actually stand on the other side you may find that that side is filled with thorns, sticks, stones, and as much manure as your side, only in different angles, degrees, and forms. So if your grass isn't growing the way you want, check first to see if you are watering, fertilizing, and grooming it the way it needs before you jump the fence. And whether it is mom's or dad's side of the coin, think about the fact that both are filled with weeds.

So Rule Number One: Communicate. Teachers teach children to give "I messages." An "I" message is a sentence which begins with "I" and helps them to express verbally, not physically, how they are feeling or thinking.

While we teach them to express their feelings, it is important to teach them to do this in socially appropriate and socially acceptable ways. Moms and Dads need to give "I" messages while also placing themselves mentally in the other parent's role to help understand the complicated task of parenting.

The "one up" contest and "I work harder than you" issues need to be cast in the arena of the dinosaur and respect, understanding, and compassion for each family member, their pressures and roles, have to be placed in center aisle.

### SUGGESTIONS:

- Moms and Dads have a "date" night, a regular night or spontaneous time for just being together.

- Moms, don't hit Dad with all of the day's problems when he walks into the door. Give him time to relax, eat, and gear back to family life.

- Dads, don't think Moms can switch from being the nurturing mom to the sexual hot spot of your desires in a matter of seconds. Foreplay to women means conversation, not the kids are asleep, a tap on the shoulder, and "How's it for you tonight?"

- Plan vacations, outings, and special time with your children and without.

- Parents, talk to each other. Trying to read someone's mind is an impossible task. Communicate your feelings, worries, and goals for yourselves and your children.

- Form a union of your parenting methods, if possible, to prevent one parent from always feeling like the "Meanie" and the other the "Fun" one. Support each other's decisions as children quickly learn how to play one parent against another, causing not only discipline problems with the child, but dissidence between the parents.

- RESPECT: as Aretha Franklin said in her music, now put it into your life. Respect the different roles and stress that accompany each role. Trade places for a few days if you need just to help you understand the different demands placed on the man and woman.

# SINGLE PARENTS AND WORKING MOMS: A DIFFERENT PLIGHT

"102 degrees" the thermometer reads. Headache, fever, nausea; the flu, you quickly diagnose. Your child looks pale and limp and the comfort of his bed and parent are the only things he wants at the moment.

Whether you are a single parent or a working mom, a sick child on an unexpected morning poses more than one dilemma. Torn between the mothering (whether you are the mother or father) you know you need to give your child, you also face responsibilities outside the home and schedule changes which may interfere with major parts of your work. For a working couple, you may have set up a pattern or schedule to take turns in these cases or the decision may rest on the plans for that specific day. You and your spouse may face a duel over whose plans are most important and whose can be changed the easiest, possibly igniting tempers and conflicts over whose job is more important, filtering on down to the ego state. For a single parent, the number of leave days designated before losing pay may be a crucial element as well as status in the job itself, depending often on the amount of understanding and leeway a particular boss allows. Fitting in a doctor's visit and taking care of the cost of his fee plus prescriptions can cause hardships on any family.

Then summer break invites additional problems for working and single parents. Although problems between the two are different, some are shared. Both groups suffer from an unrecognized disease which I shall call NETIAD; not enough time in a day.

### SPECIAL CONCERNS FOR THE SUMMER INCLUDE:

- Changes from school to child care arrangements or possible summer camp program, involves more expense (less profit from working)

- Transportation to and from activities

- Child care; worry about changes of sitters, finding responsible loving situation, child care within budget, someone to trust, proper meals, someone to love the child the way you would, safety of your child

- Struggle with "guilt" for not being home with child, not being able to participate in activities with your child

- Super mom syndrome; try to do it all

- If child care is at your home, you must think of cost and planning ahead for extra food, you may possibly face a messy house when you arrive home, other kids come over while you aren't there

- Vacation time; arrange schedules, budget for single parent may be more limited, if divorced must plan for separate time with children

- Child care restrictions; does the day care close for a week or two in the summer; or if you have a home sitter you must consider his or her vacation time

- If children are home during the day with sitter, parent may face children being bored (if child care doesn't include activities), and children may be more demanding at night for parent to entertain them

- If you rely on family for help during the summer you may be faced with your own guilt or comments from family

- If you can't afford a special summer program or your child is at an age too old for the program but not old enough to work (13-14), you may worry about activities of child during day when you aren't home. Is your child bored and watching TV all day, spending all day on the telephone, not enough supervision, friends (especially of the opposite sex) dropping by.

- Single parents may worry more about absence of other parent; children's reaction to "family vacation"

- Single fathers may face social concerns about sleep over company if he has daughters

- Restroom facilities in large public places pose a problem for opposite parents

- Young children may cry when the parent leaves adding to guilt feelings of the parent.

- 10-15 year olds may feel "too old" for child care, yet aren't responsible enough to be left alone for long periods of time and can't drive themselves to activities

- You may worry about teenagers being "left alone" too much

## TIPS

- Research all choices for child care available in your area. Day care centers offer summer camp programs, some women offer child care in their home (may or may not include activities), a sitter at home, etc. Look to find the best for your situation according to expenses, activities provided, supervision and safety factors, age of your child, etc.

- If possible try to shorten your work hours during the summer. Take only a half hour for lunch and leave earlier. See if there are parts of your job you can do at home or in the evening. Discuss with your boss some flexible options; aim for half day if you can afford it, possibly go in early (leaving the kids at home in bed with a sitter), and then leave earlier to have more of the day with them.

- Discuss your options with your children in the beginning and let them help make decisions. They'll be less likely to complain if they have some say in the choices.

- If you leave children at home with a sitter, leave a list of jobs for each day (age appropriate; unload the dishwasher, put laundry away, sweep garage, etc.).

- If you can't afford camp every week, try half day camps or alternate weeks of camp and weeks with a sitter or neighbor.

- If you have family close by, look at this option, even if for only part time help, a week or half days.

- Look for a neighborhood co-op to trade off child care. You might possibly be able to trade at night or a week end, or pay. Be sure to offer pay to neighbors for child care. Some "at home" mothers are there because they want to be but may also need the extra money.

- Try to keep your workload ahead or caught up so when that 102 degrees comes up, you aren't plagued with more guilt from a job undone.

- Plan quick menus. Older children can start simple meals before you get home. This may give you more time in the evenings to spend together.

- Look at schedules ahead of time and try to negotiate with your spouse for child care, vacation time, etc., to compromise for all.

- Single parents and working mothers may feel trapped into a rut sometimes, but try to relax. Be positive about the arrangements you make. Take time with your kids, but also take time for yourself. If money poses a restriction, remember that walking, jogging, the park, and the library are all free and can revive your spirit and your attitude during the stressful days you have. Join a support group (offered by your church, neighborhood churches or other organizations) for single parents or working mothers.

Your situation as a single parent or working mother may be difficult even though it may be by choice, but you obviously have your own set of problems. Most of all, remember your attitude is a model for your child. Your acceptance towards your situation will greatly affect your attitude. If you are upset, depressed, constantly worried or anxious your child will feel the same. Look for friends for support and send positive messages to your child about your situation. You already know from experience that your child will do as you do, not as you say. If problems begin to overwhelm you, either emotionally or financially, seek a counselor.

Life is much like a card game. Sometimes when the cards are shuffled and dealt, you get a good hand and sometimes you don't. You just have to play the best hand you can with the cards you've been dealt.

# CHAPTER 3
## I'M BORED

"MOMMMMY! I' m bored. There's nothing to do."

Your shoulder muscles flinch at the groan you hear from the stairs and you peer at the top of your child's head slowly approaching, the toes of his shoes scraping the floor as he drags them towards you. His eyes seem to be searching the carpet for answers and the frown he wears slides down his face hanging off his chin. His body slumps like a wilted flower and you catch the snarling glare from his profile shooting towards you like the pains that come with a toothache.

"There's nothing to do," he mumbles again, so low that you pretend you didn't hear while you secretly begin to plan your strategy.

His soft voice turns to a whine, much like the sound of a carrot being grated and he repeats, "Mommy, I said I'm bored. There's nothing to do."

You pause slightly, reaching deep inside for the patience and restraint you vowed you would rear your children with.

"Well, Honey, why don't you go see if your sister will play a game with you," you suggest.

"No, she's being mean to me. She just wants to talk on the phone."

"Well, one of your friends might be home. Give one of them a call."

"No, no one's at home. I already called everyone I know."

"Then go outside. You have that nice treehouse to play in."

"There's bugs up there and it's too hot," he moans.

"Well, why don't you draw or read a book," you try again.

"Mommmy! Will you play with me? You never ever play with me. Or could we go to a movie?"

"Not today, Honey, I've got a million things to do."

"But, Mommy, we haven't been to a movie in decades."

Fire begins to boil in your breath yet you feel your tongue turn to ice.

"Just go play. I'm not your entertainment guide," you hear yourself say. He bursts into tears and races upstairs. You sigh and immediately feel the guilt tug at you along with the other "to do" things on your list for the day.

One child plays well by himself, one child always has friends around, one child is always bored and you can't entertain enough!

WHAT'S A MOMMY TO DO?

# WHAT'S A MOMMY TO DO?

"Mommy! Mommy! Mommmmmmmmmy!"

*What's a mommy to do?*

*What's a mommy to do?*

*Change her name?*

*Crawl in a shoe?*

*What's a mommy to do?*

First: Take a deep breath, escape to another room and relieve stress in any private fashion of your choice, then at your leisure put the pieces back together (hopefully before danger signals ring from the other room), and make a plan.

Most importantly, talk to your child. Set some special time to spend together. Set some special time apart. Define "time apart" and be as specific as you can. Give him some choices, be fair, consistent, and enforce.

*The Bored Box:* an idea box you and your child can make together. You can make the box out of a shoe box, tissue box, candy jar, etc. You and your child both list at least 20 ideas of things to do (include both fun things and chores); then put them in the box. It's like a game. Anytime he says "I'm bored" he has to choose something out of the box. He has the choice of finding something to do on his own or choosing from the box. He has to do whatever it says, fun or a chore without complaining. This takes the pressure off of you to come up with an idea on a moment's notice and hopefully helps him learn to use his own ideas.

These are only a few suggestions. Using a positive attitude and a calm voice will reach further in all directions.

### Things You May Want to Say, May Say, But Know Not to Say

Well, you could go hang your head outside your window.

I don't care, just don't bug me.

Where' s your brain? Think for yourself.

Go get a life, kid.

Duh!

You tell me you're bored. Well, I'll make you think bored. You can sweep the floor, mop, fold the clothes and clean the bathroom like me; work, work, work, that's all I do, and you're bored.

Don't you whine and cry at me. I'll give you something to cry about.

Joking with your children can certainly ease moods and situations. Turning your child's frown into a smile is an art and helps your relationship. Laugh and joke with your child, but try to avoid sarcasm. It often comes back to haunt you.

### More Positive Possibilities

I'm sure you can think of something yourself. You have such good ideas.

Surprise me. While I finish my work you get busy, then surprise me and tell me what you did. I'll try to guess while I work.

I'd really like to play with you, but Mom's job is to finish this right now. What's your job?

Well, honey, chores are a possibility. You decide.

Don't speak; just point to the Bored Box.

### DO

Make time for yourself!

Make time for your child; read together, play a game, take a walk, ride bikes, play in the pool, go to a ballgame.

Most of all; LISTEN TO YOUR CHILD. Use limits and be reasonable.

Set a special time to share—at the dinner table—each shares a positive thing from the day.

See "Earthshattering Revelations From Moms"

---

# WHAT'S A CHILD TO DO?

Does your child sometimes remind you of the Scarecrow in the Wizard of Oz? You watch him vegetating in the middle of a room that looks like a toy store telling you he's bored and asking you what he can do.

He sings:

> "I would wile away the hours
> conferring with the flowers
> consulting with the rain
> and my head I'd be scratchin'
> while my thoughts, they'd be hatchin'
> if I only had a brain."

You secretly sing:

> "He would not be such a nothin'
> with his head all full of stuffin'
> if he'd only use his brain."

Your child does have a brain although it may often seem asleep or hidden underneath the couch potato he has become. You may have to rescue it piece by piece from the clutches of the voo doo tube, but your child can think for himself if you allow it and encourage it.

Just as a baby doesn't learn to speak if he is always handed everything he wants before he has to ask for it, and just as your foot falls asleep if you sit on it, so does your brain. Unfortunately rigid school schedules, ordered days, and after school structured activities do not foster creativity and self direction. So, give your child an adjustment period. Ease slowly into the summer routines and try to gradually eliminate ordering his day for him.

## HELPFUL HINTS

Give your child a calendar, notebook or some sort of organizer so he can record plans. For young children, use symbols or stickers and record events on the calendar together. Teach your child to record events himself rather than rely on you to keep up with his plans. Place an easily accessible and visible bulletin board for placing invitations, special reminders, a weekly calendar, etc.

## A CHILD CAN:

- think of ideas, write or list them and make an Idea Box or Jar
- make choices and decisions about activities
- learn to rely on himself for entertainment ideas
- help plan group outings
- learn to respect your life space as a person and adult
- learn manners and appropriate ways of asking
- take responsibility for own things, room and plans
- learn to expect that mom may play with him, entertain him, drive him, etc., at certain times, but other times will be designated for self directed activities

What's a child to do? He can wile away the hours. He can confer with the flowers. He can even consult with the rain. But most of all, he can stop looking for the Wizard and use his brain!

# CHAPTER 4
## LET YOUR HAIR DOWN:
## DON'T PULL IT OUT
### (Even if it is turning gray)

You feel the bobby pins pinching your temples and the tightness of your hair pulling against your scalp is forcing your head to throb. Your inclination is to pull the strands out, one by one, lifting the pressure, but a gentle pat on the shoulder stops you.

You lift your head slightly off the edge of the table. You feel the gentle pat again and soft words follow, "I love you, Mommy. What's wrong? Don't you feel good?"

Tiny wet lips press against your cheek and two dirty little arms embrace you from the side. A sloppy kiss, an awkward hug, and for reasons you don't understand, even the chocolate stain on her t-shirt softens the edge in your bite and your face melts into a smile. Instead of pulling your hair out, you lift the pins from the sides and let your hair down, falling to your shoulders. "I love you, too," you whisper.

She drags her muddy tennis shoes across the floor and the door slams behind her, but her words still echo in your mind.

Sunshine peeks through the window casting a brightness over the room. You watch your child race across the yard, skipping and singing. She grabs a small bucket and begins to collect the pine straw surrounding the trees. You and your husband worked all last week end to cover the bare ground around the trees and to make islands in the yard.

You jump to your feet. "Not there," you call from the door.

"But, Mommy, I wanna make a playhouse," she says, disappointment building in her eyes.

"But, Honey, Daddy and I just put that out last weekend so the yard would look nice."

She dumps the bucket on the ground and kicks the dirt. You watch her for a moment, then memories flash into your head.

"Hey, I've got an idea," you tell her. You find the leftover pinestraw and cart it down near the woods. "Here, you can use this," you say.

"Will you help me?" she asks.

You sigh, thinking of all the things you planned to do today. The house needs cleaning. There are phone calls to make. The book you've been trying to read is still lying on the table unopened.

"Please," she begs. Her puppy dog eyes are irrestible.

She begins to rake and push the pine straw in rows. You remember the houses you and your sister made when you were a child. Different rooms, furniture, halls, how you played for hours designing your houses and how real they became in your mind. You pick up the rake and begin helping her. The hours pass like minutes as you plan, work, talk, and laugh and as it nears lunchtime the house has a definite shape.

"I can't wait to show it to my friends. This is the greatest playhouse ever, Mom." Her face is beaming as you and she critique your labors.

"It is great!" you agree.

"I'm hungry. Can we have lunch out here?" she asks.

"Sure" you laugh, "race you."

You both pant as you get to the door, whip up sandwiches, chips, and a thermos of kool aid and carry it to your new house.

"Mommy, you can't walk through the walls," she shouts, giggling and rolling on the ground.

"I forgot," you say laughing and sprawl onto the picnic cloth.

You spread the food out onto the dining room table and light pretend candles. As you stretch out on the quilt, you realize the tension has left your body and the fresh air has cleared your head. You feel relaxed, you feel like rejoicing.

"Isn't it a beautiful day!" you say.

"The best. Thanks, Mom."

She starts a tickle fight and her giggles tell you the things words can never say. For a splendorous moment you recall a little of the reason "why you decided to have children."

# R&R:
# RELAX AND REJOICE

As you lie on the quilt you stare at the leaves. The way the wind is blowing them makes shadows against the edge of the sky. All those important "things" you needed to do today; you can't even remember some of them. You suddenly notice how some of the leaves resemble shapes of animals. On a tall branch you watch as the silhouette of one of the big leaves reminds you of a frog jumping and leaping. Suddenly you feel like a kid again. Your eyes wander from the leaves to the clouds.

"Look at the clouds," you tell your child, "doesn't that one look like a big dog and look at that one over there, it looks like two swans." Thoughts of your own childhood invade the moment and remind of you of the fun things you did as a child. But in those thoughts also creep the memories you don't have, the dreams unmet.

You never learned to roller skate but when you took your child to skate night, you tried. You felt silly at first until you noticed a few other parents struggling to keep up with their first graders. You fell a lot. You laughed a lot. You were sore for days.

You never learned to swim as a child, but when your first child loved the water, you decided to take lessons too.

You never saw the ocean as a child, yet the first time you saw it with your own child, somehow you felt you had.

You certainly can't live your life through your children's eyes completely and you certainly can't force your unmet dreams on your child to fulfill. But you can entertain life through the eyes of the child, see its freshness, recapture life's innocence and youthful spirit, and when you do, although your hair may be turning gray and your muscles may be sagging, in your heart you will feel young again.

"Priorities," you think, that was the lesson the preacher spoke of in church last Sunday. "Priorities": you decided on the most important a long time ago. Even in your most hectic moments, even in your most hurried day, your most ambitious dreams; the house, the car, the job; none can compare.

So, as they say, stop and smell the roses, count the leaves on the tree, play in the dirt, get down, but most of all: Relax, Rejoice, and Enjoy!

---

# BRILLIANT MINDS BUT SIMPLE GOALS

You graduated with honors from high school, you may have a college degree, even a Ph.D. You were voted most likely to succeed. You scored the highest in your class on the SAT. You may even have a degree and experience in teaching, but even that didn't prepare you for the strains of parenting.

You may have taken parenting classes which are offered through your local schools, counselors, churches, technical schools or community resource programs. Boundless books are available with wonderful advice on discipline, self esteem, the gifted child, the learning disabled, etc. The theories you learned were marvelous and helpful, yet there is only one problem; putting them into practice.

You, with your brilliant mind, have set brilliant goals for yourself. Now you are home with the children, you're sure you can get all the things done you want.

Yet when your husband walks in the door at dinner time, he comments, "Hey, what happened here? Looks like a tornado hit."

Hotdogs and macaroni and cheese become your five course dinner and you have sixteen projects started and none finished. You can't understand why you can't get anything done. So many goals for yourself, so many for your child that at the end of the day you feel disappointed. You feel discouraged. You feel like a failure for not getting it all done. Constant interruptions of the day light a match under your frustrations until your temper bursts into flames.

What is the problem? Perhaps, even though you are brilliant, you forgot to calculate the "NUT time factor," NUT referring to the Necessary Unexpected Times of the day. Common examples of the NUT factor include tying shoes, scrubbing dirty faces, restringing jacket strings, savoring your coffee, watching Andy Griffith reruns, cleaning spills on the carpet, the salesman on the telephone wanting you to sponsor 10 needy and underprivileged children for just $15 a month, doodling on a piece of paper, resting (what's that?), the long line at the grocery store, counting to 10 fifteen times during the day to keep your cool, chasing the dog, stopping to pick the vegetables in the garden, policing the kitchen from the neighborhood, dealing with the complaining neighbor who doesn't have children, finding the cat, finding "the" special shirt your child "has" to wear, refereeing never ending battles, transporting children to and from various friends' houses and activities, etc., and etc.

Perhaps, you have set your goals too high, too unrealistic. In doing so, you set yourself up for failure. So, as you let your hair down, lower your expectations a bit, too. Set more simple but realistic goals. A general good rule is to list three things you want to accomplish during the day, keeping in mind that the time with your kids, within limits, is your first priority on your list. List that time as a priority so you can see that it is an important accomplishment, too. Should you drop all your goals and plans for them? NO! Teaching them to value and respect your plans and goals teaches them to respect you and will later enable them to do the same for themselves as adults. When you meet the simpler goals for yourself, the feeling of accomplishment will be great. If you find you obtain those goals and accomplish yet another, what a nice surprise.

Brilliant Minds But Simple Goals; A Way To Succeed!

# WAKE UP SLEEPYHEAD,
# THIS IS THE REAL WORLD

"There's no place like home,
  there's no place like home,
  Auntie Em, Auntie Em...."

"Darling, wake up, you must have been dreaming."

"But it was the most wonderful dream. We were in the most beautiful place. We weren't in Kansas anymore. I could do whatever I wanted. I could watch TV and talk on the phone all day and stay up as late as I wanted. I could eat pizza and hamburgers and french fries and play the stereo at top volume. Nobody had to do any work or chores. It was the most beautiful and fun place you could imagine."

Our favorite stories as children "The Wizard of Oz" and "Alice in Wonderful" took us to beautiful fantasy lands. Fantasies and dreams are important for us and our children. They give us spirit and hope at times when we may not be able to see the brightness of our futures. Yet in a real family, there is the real world, too. So, dream a little dream, in your sleep or in your day dreams and don't ever forget to dream. But remember there are times when the alarm goes off, the chores have to be done, and you have to wake up sleepyhead, 'cause this is the real world!

## WHEN I WAS A KID
## Forget the Speech, Don't Ever Look Back

"Forescore and twenty years ago, our fathers before us......"

Have times really changed?

Maybe you do understand what it's like to be a kid. Maybe you haven't forgotten. Maybe you have. Even if you do, comments like these can sink to the bottom of your stomach like peach pits:

> "Everyone else I know got a car for their 16th birthday. Bill and Carl got brand new ones, too. You can't make me drive that old station wagon around. I'll be embarrassed."

> "Mom, I can't wear these old tennis shoes. They're not "in." Everyone will laugh at me. $80 is not too much for brand name shoes."

"All the girls in my class have already been dating. Why can't I?"

"Mom, can't you drive me to school. No one in 10th grade rides the school bus anymore."

"Mom, it's summer break. Summer is supposed to be for fun, not work!"

"Mom, I don't have time to do chores. It's summer. I've got to get ready to go to Tina's party and pack for camp. Then Joanie's invited me to go with her on vacation. Sorry, Mom."

"Mom, I need some money. We're going to the movies, then to get Pizza, then to play Putt Putt, then we might go for ice cream."

"You want us to clean the house? And what are you going to do, Mom, sit in the sun and read?"

"But we never have time to watch TV when school's in. I'll do my chores later."

Suddenly words stick in your throat, words hidden beneath your logic like the furballs under your bed. Saliva dribbles out of the corner of your mouth like a rabid dog and your spit feels like dragon's fire. "When I was a kid," you begin. You have an out of body experience, watching your own body deliver the speech that you detested in your own childhood.

**When I Was A Kid:**

"When I was a kid, I worked all summer, every summer. First I babysat, then mowed yards, then when I was older, I flipped hamburgers just to make enough money to put myself through school."

"When I was a kid, I never had a car! In fact, I didn't get my first car until I was married to your father and you were already born."

"When I was a kid, I never even had a store bought dress until I was in 7th grade and then only cause I had to go your aunt's wedding. I never spent $80 for a pair of shoes for me, much less you."

"When I was your age, all the girls wanted designer pocketbooks, but I never got one. I survived. It built character."

"At your age, I was already working and saving my money for college. I wasn't off riding the roads and spending every penny I had."

"I cleaned houses for people when I was twelve just to help my parents make ends meet. I never even asked for things."

"When I was a kid, I had to walk five miles to school in the snow and wear paper bags on my feet."

"When I was a kid I wouldn't have dared talk to my parents like that."

"When I was a kid, I had to take care of my little brothers and sisters for my parents to work."

"When I was a kid, no boy would have ever worn an earring."

"When I was a kid, we never went on vacations. Only thing we did was go camping a time or two. You don't know how lucky you have it."

"When I was a kid, we worked in the fields all day."

"My mama and daddy made me go to church every Sunday and you're going, too."

"When I was a kid, I started cooking supper for my mom every night before she got home from work."

"When I was a kid, we got three presents for Christmas and that was all. And you can bet we were thrilled at that. We never thought about asking for 10 or 15 things."

"Bored, how can you be bored with half of the toy store in your room? When I was a kid I would have given anything to have had all these toys. And a swimming pool in the neighborhood. Why, I never even went swimming more than once or twice when I was a kid."

### FORGET THE SPEECH! DON'T EVER LOOK BACK.

First of all, even if you've proven to your child that you were a kid once, you've shown your birth certificate, your photo album, and even shared some stories (the learning experiences of your life), his natural self-centeredness makes it difficult for him to actually believe that you know exactly how he feels. A listening ear, a supportive shoulder, an understanding (not preaching) voice is what he looks for. Certainly, his self-centeredness needs to be halted at times with rules, reminders, consequences, and perhaps short moral stories, but unfortunately the lectures and speeches often fall to angry shoulders and mother deaf ears.

Maybe you do understand. Maybe you haven't forgotten what it was like to be a fourteen year old skinny kid with braces or the little sister who got dragged to all her older brother's ballgames or even the girl who made "good grades,"got labeled as "Brains" and no boy would ask her out for a date. Maybe you haven't forgotten how bad you wanted to fit into the group. Maybe you're still trying to fit in.

Maybe you haven't forgotten what it was like to be a kid. Maybe you have. Maybe, even just a little.

Maybe you have been so busy working, worrying about finances, social responsibilities, climbing the corporate ladder, and parenting, that you have actually turned into your own mom or dad. Yikes! It's scary, but it happens.

You may find yourself uttering words you vowed you would never speak, "This hurts me more than it hurts you." "Do you want a spanking?" "Do you want me to give you something to cry about?"

Even if you have total recall of life in your early years (which is impossible after having children because half of your brain cells die with childbirth), a little truth lies in those words; "Dad, Mom, that was eon years ago." Times do change and with those changes come different pressures and stresses. Children face pressures and stresses at all times in their life according to their age. Cultural changes, socio economic levels, school systems, etc., all affect our daily lives. Pressures and stresses are all relative. They may be different for different children and in different time periods, but the real challenge is to give children the skills to cope with problems. A minor problem to you or to another less fortunate child may seem insurmountable to your child, so relatively speaking it is very important, even if it doesn't change the course of history or feed the world.

A basic constant to each child is the pot of gold for which he or she searches: parental love and approval, peer acceptance, and a love for himself. Giving your child a positive self concept, your unconditional love and support, an open ear for problems and skills to deal with problems, and the confidence and trust in himself are constants and necessities. They are your most important gift to your child, your most important achievement in life.

"How do I do this?" A seemingly impossible task, you feel at times.

Think of it as a nature hike. Some of the trail is smooth, cool and shady with very level ground, easy walking. You saunter through the path enjoying the stroll. Then you encounter stones, broken stumps, briars and occasionally poison ivy. One step at a time you make your way. Sounds just like parenting, doesn't it. You stumble over some rocks, you get scratched by the briars, a limb hits you in the face, and you reach a muddy hole. You try to jump it. Sometimes you make it. Sometimes you fall in. You clean your scratches, put bandaids on your wounds, coat yourself with Caladryl for the itching, and when you fall into the mud, you drag yourself out (a little dirtier for the wearing) but scrub your feet off, and trudge on.

So forget the speech: "When I was a Kid." Don't ever look back. The path behind you has taught you things to take with you on new trails, but to new trails you must go.

## TIPS

Teach responsibility at home. Assign chores, give choices, and let children be a part of reasonable decision making.

Privileges and consequences have to be relevant to the child and to "today," relevant to child's interests, age and meaningful. For example, if a child makes a mess, a logical consequence is to require the child to clean it up, not take his dessert away that night. Consequences should also be as immediate to the situation as possible. Punishment that is delayed for days may not have meaning to children, since they have probably already forgotten what they did to deserve it.

Ignore little unimportant things and focus on important ones. Save your issues for "real issues." Long hair or your child's shirt always being tucked in may irritate you and seem like an important issue but in the scheme of things is it so important? If you make an issue of little things it tends to damage your relationship, so save it for big things like drugs, sex, responsibilities, etc.

Use a positive approach (if you fall in the mud, crawl out, and start over). Focus on positive aspects of your child. Try not to guilt your child into doing things. A good conscience is one thing, but a guilt ridden soul is something else.

We all make mistakes, so allow yourself and your child to make them and learn from them. Show your child your mistakes. Let him see how you handle them. Remember your model is the true teacher.

Be fair, firm, and consistent. "No" is a powerful word. Use it wisely, use it well, and use it like glue, stick to it (within reason).

"WHEN I WAS A KID," "What century was that?" Your child may ask.

"Just yesterday, but a long long time ago," you say as you take his hand in yours, push through the weeds, and hike into the woods.

# THE BASIC THREE R'S:
# RIGHTS, RULES & RESPONSIBILITIES

The basic three R's: reading, writing, arithmetic: No. The basic three R's: rights, rules, and responsibilities.

Rights: You have the right to remain silent, anything you say can and will be used against you. You have the right to an attorney, if you cannot afford one, one will be appointed for you. You have the right to a speedy and fair trial. Are these the rights we speak of? No.

Although sometimes we feel like we've just been read our rights by our children and sometimes they feel the same about us, before we make the arrest and begin the fingerprinting process, hold a family meeting and discuss your rights as well as your child's.

The Constitution speaks of certain inalienable rights. In a family, both children and parents have certain rights which are dubbed rights just because of moral human nature. Obviously conflicts occur which in our social society require responsibilities to be delegated and rules to be formed in order for us to live harmoniously.

Format your family meeting as democratically as possible to encourage family participation and decision making. Children accept and follow rules and consequences better when they have had a part in the decision making. You will probably find as you and your child list your rights that many of them are the same. Although each family may list a few different rights, rules, and responsibilities, many will be basic and common. You can get as specific as you want, especially in the responsibility category.

Although, and your child will be quick to point this out, summer is a time for fun, children do have more time for chores in the summer and it is a good time to build home responsibilities.

During the school year when your child is bombarded with homework and sports or after school activities, he may not have the time to keep up with chores and you may need to alter the assigned duties so he doesn't become overly stressed. But in the summer he trades off chores for privileges and possibly transportation and extra spending money for the "fun" things he wants to do. Adapt your list to meet your family's needs.

Some suggested ones to include or think about are:

*Rights of Child:*

- right to be loved unconditionally
- right to be treated with respect
- right to be kept physically and mentally safe, clothed and fed
- right to be heard
- right to privacy
- right to be accepted for himself within his own limitations
- right to act as a child, not an adult
- right to have friends
- right to request help from parent
- right to be protected from mental or physical abuse

*Rights of Parent:*

- right to be loved
- right to be respected (although most parents find these first two rights virtually void in their children's teenage years and must accept and/or hope that in their child's early twenties these feelings will reoccur)
- right to privacy
- right to certain degree of quietness acceptable to parent's level of coping
- right to be heard

- right to make decisions which override child's choices when decisions could affect child's well being
- right to say "no"
- right to be human and make mistakes
- right to have friends and time for adult activities
- right to own personal space (such as sleep with spouse, not child)

*Responsibilities of Child:*

- responsible for own self, choices and decisions within limits of age range and circumstances
- responsible for own actions, especially those which affect others
- responsible for cleaning and caring of own belongings, room or area
- responsible for own school work
- responsible for certain chores; to be named by family
- responsible for certain amounts of money (allowance earned and spent)

*Responsibilities of Parent or Parents:*

- responsible for child's needs: love, food, clothing, shelter, physical safety, mental health
- assist children in problem solving and education
- responsible for own problems, actions, and decisions
- responsible for major decisions which affect family and well being of family members
- teach child how to do certain chores, help child learn decision making skills, values, and safety rules
- provide loving and supporting environment for child

*Rules for Child*

Be specific when possible (these are very general suggestions but you may want to discuss what each means in more specific terms). For example, discuss what constitutes "manners," asking in pleasant voice, sitting up at table, eating with silverware, etc. For each age you will have more specific rules to apply. All children need bedtime rules, toddlers need nap or rest time rules, young children need rules about picking up toys, pre teens and teenagers need telephone rules, etc.

- take care of personal things
- clean up own messes
- use quiet voice inside, loud voice outside
- run and scream outside
- respect other people's things and bodies
- use manners when asking for things and at table
- do assigned chores (decided for each individual family member, age appropriate)
- discuss with parents and obtain approval for certain activities and plans
- be honest

*Rules for Parent*

- model appropriate behavior
- approach child with positive attitude, use positive phrases
- be as consistent and fair as possible, set up rules, consequences and follow through
- be flexible when possible
- give love unconditionally and specific praise ( use phrases such as "I don't like the way you are shouting," not "You're a terrible person."
- don't blame, criticize or degrade child, especially in front of others

- treat child with respect
- do not use children as "go between" between parents
- direct discipline at "actions" or behavior, not person
- listen to your child

Once you have established your list of the basic 3 R's then it's time to move on to the "P & C's" which help you to enforce your family code on a day to day basis.

# P'S & C'S:
# PRIVILEGES AND CONSEQUENCES

Now you've compiled the law and order manual for your family, it's time to call in the enforcers—The Swat Team? NO. Superman? NO. Mom and Pop? NO. The "P's & C's" guide of your household.

"Mind your p's and q's" as the old expression says except we'll refer to them as the "P's and C's." "P's & C's" are those concrete reminders that encourage everyone to follow through.

"I'll never bribe my child," you stated before you had children. Then the moment came when you were expecting company for dinner or you were at a restaurant and you found yourself saying, "Honey, Mommy will get you a surprise tomorrow if you'll be good tonight."

Don't worry. It happens to everyone. After all, to bribe, I mean to err is human and to forgive, divine so forgive yourself; parents are people, too. Bribery does work, at least for a short time. However, if you use bribery or make deals with your child constantly you will see that as your children get older the bribes and deals get bigger and more expensive. You will soon find yourself out-foxed, out-witted, and out of money. Consider the goals you have for your children and the true lesson he or she learns from bribery. So, as you discuss the three R's with your family, make your P's & C's list to go along with it.

*Tailor Your P's & C's.* Just as you've adapted the rights, rules, and responsibilities to meet your family's needs, you must tailor the P's & C's to meet your family's needs, remembering that as your children get older you will have to readjust. Let your child be involved in setting up the privileges and consequences and let him offer suggestions for rewards.

P's & C's should be as specific as possible, age appropriate, and also as meaningful to the situation as possible. Consequences should relate to the actions.

Examples:

*Be specific.* Instead of statements like: "You're a bad girl. Behave." Say: "I don't like it when you hit your sister. If you're angry, try to use your words." Show children appropriate ways to release feelings; use words, write them down, hit a pillow, etc.

Explain what you mean by "behave" specifically.

Also, avoid statements like this: "If you ever do that again you won't see the light of day," or "The next time you hit him I'm going to knock your block off." Children do not need to be threatened and will recognize empty threats and quickly learn to ignore them.

When you begin your P's & C's list, discuss privileges and consequences (both positive and negative) for appropriate and inappropriate behaviors and carrying through of responsibilities. While you don't want to use bribery it is okay to set up positive rewards. Even adults like rewards for jobs well done.

Be as positive and specific as possible. Avoid using money or food as a reward unless the money is a set allowance for assigned chores or extra jobs. Don't pay your child to behave.

Suggested rewards: (add your own according to your child's interests)

- movies, extra TV time
- stay up later at bedtime, especially weekends
- have a friend over
- special time with parent (dinner, bike ride, walk, etc.)
- special story time or book
- choice of meal
- make special dessert
- skip a chore
- stickers (a chart system helps sometimes), when a certain number of stickers are earned a bigger reward can be given
- use of the car for teenagers

Consequences:

Make the consequence fit the behavior. For example; if a job or chore isn't done on time, the person has to complete that job and add another. If a child doesn't follow safety rules on bike, the bike must be parked for a few days. Consider time limit of consequence and be realistic or you'll cave in later.

P's & C's may seem like necessary evils sometimes but they do help to keep the crew on track so everyone has a more peaceful ride for the summer and the whole year.

More detailed books on disciplining children are found in the library and bookstores. A few suggested ones are listed in the section "Additional Resources."

# CHAPTER 5
## HOW MANY HOURS
## ARE THERE IN A DAY?

Hickory Dickory Dock
The mouse ran up the clock
The clock struck one
The kids said, "What can we do for fun?"
Hickory Dickory Dock.

Hickory Dickory Dock
The mouse ran up the clock
The clock struck two
The kids said, "Now, what can we do?"
Hickory Dickory Dock.

Hickory Dickory Dock
The mouse ran up the clock
The clock struck three
Mom said, "Go climb a tree."
Hickory Dickory Dock.

Hickory Dickory Dock
The mouse ran up the clock
The clock struck four
The kids slammed the door
Hickory Dickory Dock.

Hickory Dickory Dock
The mouse ran up the clock
The clock struck five
The baby stepped on a bee hive
Hickory Dickory Dock.

Hickory Dickory Dock
The mouse ran up the clock
The clock struck six
"Let's make the brownie mix"
Hickory Dickory Dock.

Hickory Dickory Dock
The mouse ran up the clock
The clock struck seven
Mom said, "The dishes are stacked to heaven"
Hickory Dickory Dock.

Hickory Dickory Dock
The mouse ran up the clock
The clock struck eight
The dog's licking the plate
Hickory Dickory Dock.

Hickory Dickory Dock
The mouse ran up the clock
The clock struck nine
Mom said, "I'm losing my mind"
Hickory Dickory Dock.

Hickory Dickory Dock
The mouse ran up the clock
The clock struck ten
"WILL THIS DAY EVER END?"
Hickory Dickory Dock.

# THE ARSENIC HOUR

"Working 9 to 5, trying to make a living, 9 to 5." Your job may be out of your home or in your home, but when the 5 o'clock buzzer goes off and you are a parent, you are still on duty.

You step into the kitchen to begin dinner. Your stomach is already growling and you feel fatigue sweeping over you. A short rest on the couch, your feet up, a cold drink, and a quiet few minutes could just rejuvenate you. But do you have the time? If you don't have children most probably. If you do have children probably never. The baby crawls behind you tugging at your leg. The toddler is climbing onto the counter begging for a cookie. The kids need to be fed either for pressing activities or for baths and a reasonable bedtime. Your spouse is due home soon, and the phone is ringing with salesmen just waiting for the hour when most people are home, so that restful break you need seems to be postponed with the other personal delicacies of life. As soon as you enter the kitchen you are bombarded with "What's for dinner, Mom? OOH, I don't like that. Can't we just have pizza." The pot begins to boil. Someone screams from upstairs. The baby drags all your pots and pans from the cabinet. The doorbell rings. The buzzer from the dryer goes off. The dog knocks over the plant. The toilet overflows. An injured one appears bleeding at the kitchen door needing band aids, and sibling warfare breaks out in the den. Your spouse walks in to see a floor full of pots, pans, and tupperware, one child hanging on your leg, screams from the entire house, make up dripping off your chin and the smile he needs to see after his hard day's work is disguised as despair. THE ARSENIC HOUR! It happens in every household to differing degrees but the continuing saga of the 4–7 time slot in a family type household characterized as the arsenic hour is profound.

As profound as this phenomenon is, a few tips can help ease (though never cure or totally eliminate) the discomforts of this hour. Tired and hungry parents, tired and hungry kids; the natural lull in our bodies greets us at a time that demands us to keep busy. Our bodies and minds beg for peace and rest, but the baby is still clinging to the mom's leg, the toddler is still destroying the house, and the adolescent is still making plans so the arsenic hour must be prepared for.

## TIPS

- Young ones, especially infants to four years, usually need a nap or rest time after lunch. Use this time for all the "Have to's" you need to do, but try to schedule in a few minutes rest and peace for yourself. Look at a magazine, write a letter, close your eyes and nap yourself, do a craft, whatever helps relax you and gives you therapy.

- A small snack for children in the afternoon can help tide them over until dinner. Try to set a regular time to avoid a marathon snack time which could interfere with dinner appetites.

- Turn the answering machine on during arsenic hours. Listen to the machine and answer only when you choose.

- Adjust meal times depending on your children. Sometimes it's not worth listening to the toddler whine for an hour to wait for a "family dinner." Occasionally feed the kids early, put them to bed, and have a quiet dinner with your spouse.

- Establish a rule for older children. When I cook you play outside. This is your reading time, board game time, chore time, etc., (whatever works for you and your family).

- Young children want to be close to you (no matter how hard you try to arrange otherwise), so arrange your cabinets for safety. Fix a couple of cabinets with pots and pans or plastic wear for them to play in while you cook. Give containers and spoons for pretend play. Dry macaroni provides stimulating play and entertainment for the young cook.

- When your patience allows, let your child help cook. Young children can do simple tasks like washing vegetables, tearing lettuce, setting the table, etc. Older ones can chop and mix.

- Prepare parts of the meal early in the day. While your child watches his favorite TV show, colors a picture or reads, mix up a casserole or put something in the crock pot. Preparing ahead takes a little more thinking and planning but can save you much anxiety later in the day.

- A glass of wine or a cold drink can help relax you, even a small snack for yourself can take the edge off as you cook.

- Music; either your favorite tape or the radio can soothe you and children also.

- Unless being a gourmet cook is your dream, throw off your Julia Child image and prepare simpler meals than before you had children. Children generally eat plainer foods versus fancy casseroles and sauces. Less time in the kitchen will mean more time with your child in pleasant circumstances.

- When you have leftovers, fix them on a plate, freeze and have ready to heat for rushed times. You can even prepare casseroles ahead of time and freeze, then use later.

- Fresh vegetables are more nutritious, especially if they are steamed and left slightly crisp (so the nutrients aren't totally drained). However, frozen vegetables are handy for quick dinners and fresh fruits are easy and nutritious.

# NIGHT, NIGHT ANGEL

"Rock a bye baby
in the tree top
when the wind blows
the cradle will rock
When the bough breaks
the cradle will fall
Down will come baby
cradle and all."

"Rock a bye baby
all through the night
When the dawn comes
I'll look such a sight.

If you don't sleep
Now what will I do?
So stay in your bed
the whole night through."

"Isn't she precious, lying there sleeping so peacefully?" your husband whispers to you, reaching out to touch her back.

You nod, smiling, then grab his hand forcing it away from her. "Yes, dear, but it took me an hour to get her to sleep so please don't wake her up."

The door slams from the bathroom. "Mom, I'm hungry? What's for breakfast?"

"Wha- wha" goes the baby.

Fatigue sweeps over you and you drop your head in despair. "Your turn to get the little angel to sleep," you mumble to your spouse, drag your feet back to your room and lunge your body across your bed. The clock says 6 o'clock. You had hoped to have the baby asleep by five and grab another hour of much needed sleep before your other one awoke, but no such luck. Your nights run into mornings, your mornings stretch into nights. Your eyes have taken on the zombie look and even cakes of make-up have trouble masking your dark circles.

With older children, your summer nights may be filled with swim meets, ball games or other activities you've been saving for "summer," or waiting up (or sleeping with one ear open) for teenagers who are testing the curfew. Summer often means late nights, trips, and spending the night with friends which all involve a change in schedule. This often results in a tired mom and tired children.

You can't totally eliminate the problem without becoming too rigid, something which school necessitates but which summer was fashioned for, more flexibility. What can you do though to minimize the destruction when the imbalance of fatigue captures you and your children and crumbles you into pieces like broken crackers?

## TIPS

- First, expect summer to be different and try to go with the flow as much as possible.

- Establish a routine for preparing for bed; bath, snack, story time, music, water, bathroom, five minutes of lying with you and whispering (whatever you and your child choose). Routines are very important for younger children to mentally unwind them and help calm them for bedtime. Older children may also need some form of routine, especially if they have trouble falling asleep. A set bedtime (as flexible as you can be), seems important for people with any type of sleep problem. A warm bath also helps to relax.

• Once you have said good night and left your child's bedroom, try not to go back. Set up your rules and stick to them. Give your child ample time with you in the room to say his good night, story, kiss, water, etc., but be firm that when you leave the room he is to stay in his bed and go to sleep. If he repeatedly comes out of the room after you've left, discuss the problem with him. Ask his suggestions. Set up a chart to list times when he does (be positive) stay in his bed and reinforce the behavior you desire. Use a reward system to follow up.

• If your child always has a "stomach ache," is afraid, upset or worried, or always has something else he forgot to tell you about, leave a blank pad, journal or notebook in his room with a pencil or crayon. He can draw or write about it and leave it for you to see in the morning, rather than calling you or getting up. Give him a "worry book" to write in or set a special time to talk about worries.

• Quiet activities before bedtime help calm children. For example, reading, TV, quiet games, etc. Too many activities and too much physical exercise can stimulate children.

• Avoid foods and beverages with caffeine such as chocolate, sodas, etc. Avoid candy and foods high in sugar late in the evening also. Both caffeine and sugar stimulate children and cause difficulty in sleep patterns. However, a nutritious snack or glass of milk may help the child to go to sleep.

• Babies may need an extra bottle, rocking, or a soft back rubbing to calm them. As the baby gets older, if he wakes up, try not to get in the habit of getting him up and rocking him.

Pat his back softly or play soft music in the background. A night light may help infants and young children who may not like the dark.

- Avoid TV or stories that might frighten children in the evening.

- If children plan to sleep together or share a room on vacation and don't normally do this, have a practice run a couple of nights before you go to help them get used to it. Leave a few books or pad and crayons for one to use if he wakes up first, instead of waking the other.

- Try to get adjoining rooms in hotels or a condo with separate rooms for children and adults. You'll be miserable if you are sitting in a hotel room with the lights off at 9:00 waiting for your child to fall asleep. He's in a strange place and will probably take longer to fall asleep and you aren't ready for bed yet so tensions may easily rise to the surface.

- Try to get your child (especially babies and young children) used to sleeping in different places; at a friend's, neighbor's, or grandma's so when vacation time comes it won't be his first. Take a porta crib or bedrail with you if your child is used to having one. Check for child proofing in each place you visit.

- Think of your individual children and the amount of rest each requires when establishing bedtimes. Each child is different, may need different amounts of sleep and may handle lack of sleep differently. This becomes difficult if an older child actually needs more sleep than a younger child for this can become a real issue; age and bedtimes. Try to make compromises but be firm about rest. Try to put the responsibility on your child. Remind him of activities that he needs to be rested for such as sports, music, etc.

- Young children often like a special blanket or toy to sleep with. When traveling or spending the night out, take it with you. Often children sleep better with their own pillow.

- If your plans require a "late night," establish a rule about a rest time the next day or an earlier bed time to "catch up." Young children may need a nap time on vacation daily (especially if they do at home) or if their schedules have gotten too off balance.

- If your child has trouble falling asleep at a reasonable bed time, evaluate his daily schedule. The toddler may no longer need a long nap, he may be oversleeping in the morning, the teenager may want to sleep all day and stay up all night. Your child may be lying around all day watching TV and not using any physical energy.

- If your child chooses bedtime as a time to become anxious about things, think about problems, etc., help him learn to do that at another time. Give him a journal or book to write worries in before bedtime so that he doesn't take them to bed with him. Have a special talking or sharing time before he goes to bed so he can voice any problems or share information so bedtime isn't prolonged. Each family has to adapt according to the lifestyle of the family.

- If your child wakes up at night and comes into your room, comfort but take him back to his room. If the problem persists, check with your doctor to make sure there isn't a medical reason (such as ear aches, teething, etc.) for your child waking up. If there isn't and if the problem becomes a pattern, try to encourage your child to sleep in his own bed all night. For older children, set up a chart and reward system that your child can actively record and keep up with. With infants, you may need to let them cry for a few minutes and learn to fall back asleep themselves. Usually, the first night the infant may cry heavily, but each night it should improve. This takes patience and strength on your part but sometimes proves to be the only way to train them. If a serious problem continues with any age child, consult your pediatrician. Sometimes sleep problems are due to medical problems, other times stress can trigger them. Try to look for the cause and treat as well as working to establish set patterns.

- Although summer calls for more flexible hours, later bedtimes and schedules, remember also that your spouse probably still goes by his same work schedule. Respect his right for some quiet time at night. Mom will still need that time alone with Dad so even if children aren't asleep at the regular time, require them to watch TV, read or play a game in their own room.

- If your family's patterns have slipped into later bedtimes and later mornings for the summer, remember to gradually ease back into the earlier schedules a week or two before school starts back to help the transition.

## RAIN, RAIN GO AWAY

"Rain, rain go away
Come again another day
Little children want to play."

You awake with your optimistic morning attitude (attempted anyway), to the sound of drip, drip, drop, thunder and pop. "Okay" you think, still lying in bed. You and the kids could all use a break from the torture of the sun. Sun screen is expensive, the kids' hair is turning green from chlorine, and your washing machine needs a break from wet towels. The yard needs rain, the grass is turning brown, the flowers you worked so hard to plant are wilting, the county has a water ban for outside watering and you know you are long over due for a rainy summer day. You snuggle under the covers and listen to nature's watering can sprinkling the earth and doze for a few more minutes. It's always so nice to sleep when it's raining, you think as you drift into a pleasant morning dream.

Shortly thereafter, you awake to the roaring of thunder and a bed full of children cuddled beside you. You snuggle and cuddle for a few minutes, but soon the restless bodies beg you for food.

"What are we going to do today?" the first one asks before you climb out of bed.

"Yeah, we can't go to the pool today."

"Oh, rainy days are good for lots of projects," you begin. "We can clean the closets, and organize the toy shelves, and play games."

Your bedroom is suddenly clear of children. It's amazing, just mentioning "work" produces the scattering and hiding of bodies in your household.

Spoons and bowls clatter in your kitchen as the children treat themselves to the hordes of sugary cereal housed in the cupboard. Chairs screech across the floor as the kids exit the table and dutifully carry their bowls to the sink. Unsmiling faces grunt at you behind milk mustaches left over from breakfast.

"We don't wanna clean!" The protests begin.

In spite of their protests, you manage to coerce them into helping and after a short while everyone seems enthralled in the process of organization, stopping to play with toys and games they hadn't noticed in months. A hard day's work, new found old toys, lunch, TV, board games, a few minor arguments, but you and the kids survive the rainy day.

Day 2: You awake once again to the musical parade of raindrops on the roof and you begin to sing a little tune:

> What can we do on a rainy day, rainy day, rainy day,

What can we do on a rainy day, when we can't go out to play?

We can build with blocks on a rainy day, rainy day, rainy day,

We can build with blocks on a rainy day, when we can't go out to play.

We can do puzzles on a rainy day, rainy day, rainy day,

We can do puzzles on a rainy day, when we can't go out to play.

You continue the song throughout the day, especially at lulls in the entertainment department, encouraging the children to fill in the answers. Cartoons, washing and redressing all the baby dolls, an outing for lunch, a rented movie, make milkshakes in the afternoon, pull out the watercolors and paint, chores, the library, build a block city, finally dinner time. (How many hours were there in this day?)

Day 2: survived.

Day 3: (Tune of 10 little Angels)

There was one, there were two, there were three little raindrops,

There were four, there were five, there were six little raindrops,

There were seven, there were eight, there were nine little raindrops,

A hundred little raindrops on the roof.

"Not again!" you hear the groans across the hall. You roll over and pretend to be asleep when the tiptoes enter your room.

"Mom, it's raining again."

"Yeah, we're sick of it. Why does it ALWAYS have to rain?"

This time you grunt, "Go watch TV." You reprimand yourself silently for sending them to the voodoo tube, drag yourself into the shower, and frantically search your brain for another 16 hours worth of childhood entertainment ideas.

The skating rink for some physical activity, a movie, pizza out. The grocery store on the way home for junk food. The children race in the house and head straight for the linen closets. Someone suggested building tents and forts on the way home and in spite of your objections, they detailed the plans as you drove into the driveway. You haven't the energy to argue when you notice the blankets, sheets,and towels being drug from the closet and draped into tents. "Well, they have to play," you tell yourself and resign yourself to the idea of Cyclone City.

Day 3: survived, a little testy, exasperated and exhausted, but survived.

Day 4: The children stand over your bed in a chorus of:

> It's raining,
> It's pouring,
> This rain is getting boring!

Cabin fever in winter time was a struggle, but at least the kids had school or preschool. These lazy hot summer days, couch potatoes watching reruns and the same movie over and over, the pitter patter of the pouring rain and running footsteps through your house is driving you crazy.

You drop to your knees and pray:

> Rain rain, go away
> Please let the sun shine today
> My children desperately need to go out and play
> Or their mommy may just run away.

## RAINY DAY ACTIVITIES

• Research your library, bookstores, educational school supply stores and catalogs for specific activity books for children. Keep a book on hand for last minute ideas.

• Utilize tapes, records, and songs on rainy days. Valentine Productions produces a specific tape entitled, "Rainy Day Activities."

• Utilize toys you have on hand. Rearrange and organize them. Search for games you haven't played with in a while.

• Set up time for you and your child to play or work together, a time also for independent entertainment or play (child must play alone or with siblings to give you a break).

• Read children's magazines such as Highlights or Cricket. They are filled with stories, activity pages, and craft ideas.

• Check sources such as libraries, neighborhood art centers and recreation centers for ideas and programs. Check local newspapers for listings of movies, museums, exhibits, puppet shows, and other local interest activities.

• Set up a work time; clean rooms, or playroom, organize toys, clothes, games, etc.

• Make a special game or reading time: set up a story place or game area, use sleeping bags, special snacks, etc.

• Prepare special snacks or foods, let the children help choose and read recipes, cook or prepare.

• Sing "What can you do on rainy day" and let the children list activities they would enjoy. Then choose.

• Start making Christmas projects (December is always too busy anyway); needlepoint, painting ornaments, stenciling, etc.

- Teach your child to sew or cook, build with wood, a new craft or skill. Make small pillows, doll clothes, a blanket for a teddy bear, bird houses, doll houses, ramps or garages for small cars.

- Read a book or story and act it out. Choose a story, play, or song, and make up a dance or act it out. Invite friends to help or watch. Make simple props and costumes.

- Read, read, read. Everyone might want to choose a favorite book and tell about it at dinner.

- Have a scavenger hunt inside.

- Set a goal: try to play with every toy or every game you have before the rain stops.

- Paint; use watercolors on paper, craft paints for t-shirts, socks, hats, etc. Explore different kinds of painting; fingerpainting, paint with jello pudding or shaving creme (this cleans tables wonderfully), paint with Q-tips or sponges, marble paint, straw paint, soapflake paint. Color bubbles and blow on paper to make bubble pictures.

- Cut and paste pictures from construction paper. Gather different items such as cloth, ric rac, buttons, seeds, lace, yarn, cotton, different kinds of cereal, etc., and glue on paper to make a collage.

- Make sandboxes for play out of tubs with flour, cornmeal, noodles. Play, measure, write in, draw, use small plastic animals, dinosaurs, etc.

- Color noodles with food coloring; let dry, string to make necklaces or glue on paper and design pictures. Label "Nutty Noodles."

- Try some simple science experiments. Make Rainbow in a Jar; mix food coloring and water in jar and watch colors mix. Make an Ocean in a Jar. Mix baby oil, blue food coloring, and water in glass jar or bottle (with lid), add sand, small shells and plastic fish. Watch the waves as you tilt the bottle from side to side.

- Use hammer and nails and make a woodworking project from scrap lumber.

- Make instruments from cans or pie tins. Fill with beans or pop-corn seeds, cover and decorate. Then play with favorite songs and have a marching band.

- Study recycling. Organize recycling bins if you haven't already. Read and use ideas from *52 Ideas to Save Your Earth.*

- Use rocks you have collected: look for books about rocks, read, sort and try to label or name ones from your collections. Also choose a special rock to paint or decorate.

- Pick an animal or country that you are interested in. Go to the library and find books on it and bring home and read. Make a list of all the things you learn about it.

- Plan a rainy day party or picnic: invite friends and set up games, indoor picnic (include ants on a log, peanut butter spread on celery sticks with raisins on top for ants), put little paper umbrellas in the Kool-Aid. May also have bear picnic (use any theme, dinosaur, turtle, etc.) and let everyone bring that item. For example, bear picnic, serve bear cookies, have a bear hunt, tell scary bear stories, etc.

- Bathe and wash all the toy dolls in the house, dress and fix their hair.

- Build a parking lot for all the toy cars, assign parking spaces. Make roads and highways. Label. Draw a map of your finished city.

- Build with legos, blocks, etc. May need to give suggestions to children.

- Designate the day as "Mexican Day" or "Hawaiian Day," etc. Prepare foods of that state or country, art, dress. Find stories from the library about the state or country. Visit a travel agency for brochures and pictures.

- Organize your family photo album.

- Have a pretend camping trip; children make tents and forts from sheets. Make S'mores for snacks. Draw things you might see in the woods. Make pretend campfire and tell stories. Take a pretend hike through the house. Look for anything made from nature—flowers, designs, baskets, etc.

- Use old shoe boxes and make dioramas; use small playdough or plastic animal figures (ex.; dinosaurs, farm animals) or small cracker animals like goldfish, add paper cut outs, straw, rocks, etc.

- Use an old sock and other scrap material and make a puppet.

- For young children, use cereal, teddy grahams, goldfish, fruit snacks in different shapes, sizes, and colors. Count sort, classify and make patterns with the different foods.

- Gather different kinds of seeds; compare, plant in cups inside. Let child take care of them. Later transfer to outside.

- Play and share some old games such as Musical chairs, hot potato, charades, bingo, Pictionary.

- Write stories, illustrate and make into your own books.

- Do experiments with water. Measure, pour, freeze, heat, etc. Look for books about rain and study about the clouds. Go to the library and research average number of inches of rainfall in your area, other areas, chart which areas have the most, least, etc.

- Take a field trip to a nature store or museum.

- Collect rain in a bucket. Measure. Pretend it is a wishing well and make up stories about what you would wish for.

# ARE WE THERE YET?

"99 bottles of coke on the wall, 99 bottles of coke, take one down, pass it around, 99 bottles of coke on the wall, 98 bottles of coke on the wall, 98 bottles of coke, ... a million more miles to go in the car, a million more miles to go, if we don't get there very soon, out the window one will go."

The car is filled with gas, the insides are bulging to the seams like overstuffed pillows, and your city limit sign is still visible when the first "Are we there yet? How much longer 'til we get there?" begins.

You buckle your seat belt, study the map, check your watch, and choke on your own words, "Oh, just a little bit further. Just relax and enjoy the ride."

ENJOY THE RIDE! If you really expect that, you have never experienced riding in the car with young children for any time longer than four minutes, have never been subjected to endless backseat bickering, and have not yet been indoctrinated into the full realm of parenthood. Only after you have traveled with your own children can you sincerely appreciate your own parent's courage in taking you on vacation.

Beware though, you as a parent can do a few things to lessen the stress and strife you are about to undertake. Unfortunately sedating your children is not an alternative, so live with them you must. Prepare for your travels and your journey may be tolerable; forget to prepare and you may find your vacation cancelled before you use your first tank of gas.

## TIPS

- First, make sure your automobile is mechanically healthy and safe before you start. This includes brakes checked, tires, oil, etc.

- Make sure you have a first aid kit, spare tire, flashlight, jack, and jumper cables with you. While car phones seem like a luxury for the business world, they can be useful for emergencies, so if you can afford it, invest in a portable one. (Then it can also be carried to other vehicles).

- Carry a blanket in the trunk in case you get stranded, (especially in cold climates).

- Carry a garbage bag in the car for trash (one per day of travel). A roll of paper towels and wipes come in handy also.

- Establish your "travel" rules before you begin. Set up a reward system (small stickers, stamps, candy: M & M's) if you feel you need it. Talk about car manners, expectations, and consequences. If bickering gets out of hand, stop the car, and wait until things cool down.

- Plan your trip and investigate locations of cities, distances, hotels, etc. Make reservations in advance. Chart on map and let the kids help you. Also, list and mark on your map any "interest" items on your journey, especially good stopping points; the MacDonald's with the playground, the tiny mall with the merry go round, the unusual baseball card shop; any place that might be an interesting side stop to break up the trip. Make small flags from toothpicks and construction paper triangles to mark the places you visit. Count the number of counties, states, etc., that you pass through.

- Consider rush hour traffic times in major cities and plan to avoid.

- Plan for a longer travel time to allow plenty of time for stops. The kids and you need bathroom, food, and exercise stops. Also change places in the car after stops. This alleviates some monotony.

- Stop BEFORE the children are starved. A 20 minute wait turns into dreadful hours when you find yourself on a long stretch of highway with hungry kids.

- Let each child take a pillow to rest on and possibly nap with. Children often sleep better in strange places if they have their own pillow. Each child also can choose one favorite toy or blanket to take for security.

- Pack a bag of snacks for the car or plane, preferably dry snacks for less mess. Juice boxes or pouches will be more nutritious than sodas.

- Limit intake of drinks, especially soft drinks, to lessen the number of bathroom stops and also the sugar kick. Avoid candy and lots of sweets as they tend to hype children up.

- Let each child pack a bag of activities for the ride. For example, small handheld video games, Game Boys, travel board games, crayons and paper (avoid markers), magic slates, word search, mad lib, and activity books, books for reading, car bingo games, card games, tapes, etc. Toy and department stores carry a variety of travel games, some with magnetic pieces.

- Include music tapes, story tapes, a radio with ear phones. Valentine Productions produces a tape "Games For the Road" available in catalogs and stores. Song tapes are also available at toy stores and book stores.

- Beware of children who experience motion sickness. Curvy roads and air travel cause problems with many children. Take a bottle for the baby, candy, life savers, gum, and possibly motion sickness pills for older children. Keep car air circulating. A dry snack such as crackers may also help.

- When listening to the radio or tapes as a family, let each person have a turn to choose the tape.

- Have a "let loose, sing along, silly time" with songs or jokes, then "quiet times for rest" for both the children and your sake.

- Before your trip make a list of things you might see. Take with you and when you see the item, check it off or record it. At the end of the trip you can count and see how many things you found. Make a new list for the way home.

- If possible, make stops at parks, food establishments with playgrounds, or picnic areas to give everyone a chance to get fresh air and run around.

- On long trips, you may want to wrap small surprises and let your child open a present every hour.

- Divide in teams; two sides of car. Look for and count the number of certain items. Suggestions: number of farms, vans, trucks, graveyards, rivers, etc.

- Punch buggy or Slug bug game; when a person spots a VW he calls punchbuggy or slug bug and the color. He then gets to "lightly" punch anyone in the car wearing that color.

- Play I SPY.

- Play word games. Tell the children anytime you say the word "Car" while driving they should say "Wheel." Make up other words to include in the game.

- Grocery Store or (any kind of store), child pretends to have store, thinks of item in store that begins with certain letter, other child guesses; one who guesses gets the next turn.

- Play other word games, such as listening for rhyming words, beginning letters, etc.

- Read aloud a story and talk about it. Short picture book type stories are best for young children. Include old folk tales, then make up different endings. Chapter books are great for older kids. Try to read a chapter every 100 miles. Poetry is also fun. *The Light in the Attic* and *Where the Sidewalk Ends* by Sid Silverstein are excellent books of poetry for children. Children can make up their own poems also. Make up nonsense words or read funny joke books to entertain everyone in the car.

- Each child can take a small diary or journal to record events of the trip. Have them write in it once every hour.

- For babies, be sure to plan ahead for meals. Take extra bottles, formula, dry baby food already measured in plastic container or bag. Restaurants will usually heat bottles or provide hot water for baby food if you request.

- Alphabet Game: Look for places, signs and license plates that start with certain letters. Call out or play silently. Begin with A, then go to Z.

- Hold breath when pass graveyard, hold feet up when cross over railroad tracks, hold finger in air, feet up, and hold breath when pass over bridge.

- Make a story train. One person in the car starts a story with one sentence. Take turns going around and each person adds a sentence to tell more about the story. Tape on a small cassette and listen back.

- At rest areas, look for brochures about the different places you are visiting. Children love to look at these and plan site seeing while on the road.

- Take a camera and teach the children how to take pictures. For younger children give them a toy camera. Also a pad of paper for drawing the things they see can be turned into a photo album book as you travel.

- For very long trips, set goals for short periods of time. Make a plan. For example, the first hour we will sing along, mark off with sticker or stamp each hour, the second hour we will play games, third hour we eat, take an exercise break, fourth hour (after lunch) rest, quiet music or read, etc. Give some kind of reward or mark off your goal as you reach it.

- Most rules for car travel apply to air travel. However, when planning to fly, try to make advance reservations so your family sits together. If possible ask for the bulkhead seats to give your family more leg room and a place for kids to sit and play. Avoid sitting by the wing as it blocks a child's view. If you're nursing a baby, request a back seat for more privacy and quiet. Use gum, candy or a bottle to ease ear pain from air pressure. Try to arrange for nonstop or direct flights. Any change of planes can cause distress as it often leads to families with strollers, luggage and children rushing to make connections or possibly missing connections and having a long layover. Include snacks and lap toys as you do in the car.

# HOMEBOUND OR LOONY BOUND?

"Mom, what are all these little red bumps? They itch."

"You look like you've got polka dots," the younger sibling says, pointing to the mounds of red blisters popping out all over your older child's body like popcorn exploding in the microwave.

"Mom, he's laughing at me. It's not funny, it itches!"

You examine your child's body and yes, to your dismay, the itchy itchy chicken pox plague has begun. If you have more than one child you quickly do a mental count down of the days of exposure, length of illness and figure that you have anywhere from 2 to 6 weeks of this itching, scratching, scabby, feverish, irritable child-hood disease to contend with. Homebound, yes! Loony bound by the end of the first day, maybe.

Whether you and your child are homebound by chicken pox, another illness such as asthma, a broken limb, surgery, or any other illness, there are times when children's activities will be restricted.

Your child may be restricted to complete or partial bedrest or simply limited to quiet activities. Although you will inevitably begin caring for your child as the legends of Florence Nightingale and the mother of the Brady Bunch have inspired you, you may soon feel like Count Dracula would obviously feel if the world had 24 hours of constant daylight. A caged lion hunting for food in a health food store may have more patience than you after days of indoor television, soup, lack of sunshine, and a whining unhappy child.

Serious illnesses or hospitalization may require mostly love, prayers, and medical assistance which are both physically and mentally exhausting and stressful. However, when your child rides that line of being well enough to be bored but not well enough for physical activities, you face a different challenge.

So, before you completely resign yourself to join the Loony Tune crowd, keep these helpful hints in your repertoire of survival tactics.

## TIPS

- In any situation, try to keep yourself rested. This is difficult when an illness requires around the clock supervision or if a child is simply not sleeping well, but grab much needed rest when you can. Trade off with a spouse or supportive friend or relative when possible to help you keep your strength. Physical exhaustion drains you and hinders your positive attitude and patience with your child.

- Avoid skipping meals as this may add an extra strain on your body which during stressful times needs extra food for energy.

- Exercise daily, even if only for a short time. Vigorous exercise or a simple walk will help you feel better both mentally and physically and relieve stress.

- Allow time to yourself. Whether your child is bed bound or simply restricted, plan certain times of the day to spend with him, but also set up a time for him to rest or entertain himself while you do the same for yourself.

- Expect irritability and try to be understanding, but don't accept verbal abuse from your child. Ignore as much as possible and try to help your child direct to the positive instead of dwelling on his illness or restrictions.

- Set obtainable goals with your child. For example, if your child is confined for ten days, have a calendar and mark the days. Set up small reachable goals. For instance, mark off every two days and reward to help your child when you meet the goals so he can feel some accomplishment and not feel overwhelmed by the length of time.

- Encourage visits or phone calls from friends or family if your child is physically able. Set time limits, if needed, to give your child the appropriate amount of rest. Establish the time limits before the phone call or visit to avoid distress at the end of the call or visit.

- Each morning or evening, your child or the two of you together, can make a list of activities for the day or following day. Let him help plan. Just thinking of things to do will help motivate him and pass the time. Also, recap at the end of the day and talk about which activities you enjoyed the most.

- Let your child keep a journal or diary of this time. He can write anything he chooses, read with you or keep private.

- Provide a lap top pillow desk, TV tray or other small tray type table for the bed (ones especially for children are available at toy stories or discount department stores), for writing, drawing, playing games, etc.

- Chart your child's progress to help him see his own improvements.

- Spend time talking with your child. Also use storytelling from books, favorite stories, or stories of your childhood to entertain him. You may want to make up stories with your child. Choose a favorite toy or animal and create your own story. Write the story down or record on a small cassette and play back. Children also love to hear stories of things they did when they were smaller, include expressions they said, faces, reactions to certain things, etc.

- For young children, read to or with your child. Some children and older children may want short stories, magazines, or a long novel to read themselves.

- Art projects are great entertainers. Choices range from simple drawings and coloring projects to card and gift making to elaborate craft projects. Provide supplies and let your child create his own ideas.

- Activity books, dot to dots, sticker books, hidden pictures, crossword puzzles, and word search books are available in stores and can provide hours of entertainment.

- Provide age appropriate games such as checkers, Candy Land, Monopoly, Scattergories, etc., puzzles, tapes, paper dolls, toys, sewing projects, building blocks (legos are great!), small manipulatives for young children, projects such as models for older ones, experiments or a book about something of your child's interest or hobby if he has one.

- Prepare simple skits or programs for the family such as puppet shows (make your own puppets or use ones you already have), magic shows, renditions of favorite stories or movies, etc.

- Set up work type centers and let your child play. For example, provide with medical materials such as gauze, a toy medical kit and let your child pretend to be a Dr. Other suggestions: hair dressing; use combs, brushes, rollers, etc. and style hair or doll's hair. Office: use typewriter, computer, staples, hole punch (children love to punch holes with a hole punch; let them make their own design), paper and note cards.

- Organize and label family pictures into albums or make a special album for each child, letting your child pick out the pictures to go in each book.

- Organize collections such as baseball cards, rocks, ribbons or certificates your child has received, etc.

- Make special snacks. Let your child help if possible and be creative. For example, food art; string fruit loops to make a necklace, make snowmen out of marshmallows and raisins, make blue jello for the ocean and put in shark bite fruit snacks for a summer snack.

- Utilize the rainy day activity section or craft magazines and books for ideas of specific projects.

# CHAPTER 6
## PLEASE, PLEASE,
## JUST A FEW MINUTE'S PEACE!

You've folded five loads of laundry each day for weeks, swept the floor nonstop, served 12 meals and 16 snacks a day, suffered through skating with your own children plus half the neighborhood who needed a ride, seen every child's movie in town since the rain began 13 days ago, and PMS is setting in. All this quality time you yearned for seems to be turning into endless mindless tasks, arguments, and you've found yourself insisting that it is your turn to get the prize out of the cereal box. You have forgotten your name, if you ever owned one other than Mom and you secretly fantasize yourself driving down the highway in the smallest convertible you can find (something you couldn't possibly carpool in), listening to your favorite tape at full blast, and screaming profanities. You momentarily gain control, long enough to lock yourself in the bathroom (for your own children's safety, you remind yourself), and relieve your tongue of the distasteful words plaguing you. As you sit there, the children bang on the door shouting, "Mommy, Mommy." You beg, "PLEASE, PLEASE, JUST A FEW MINUTES PEACE!"

## TOO MUCH TOGETHERNESS

However weak your language may be at this point, since the main conversation you have engaged in over the last few weeks consists of "What's for dinner?" "There aren't any good snacks," "Please pick up your mess" and "Shut the door! The air conditioning is on!," you feel certain that other words still exist in the English language and that there are other people outside the world communicating. Last night you cut your husband's meat for him at dinner, sorted your M & M's by color before you ate them, shouted "Mine" when your neighbor asked to borrow something, dreamt about the muffin man, and sang "Hush, little baby," in your sleep. Aha! TOO MUCH TOGETHERNESS! No one ever told you what twenty four hours of parenting a day, seven days a week could do to a person.

The children go out with their friends, you know because you spend half your day arranging it and driving them to and fro. So, why shouldn't you? After all, remember, parents are people, too. You grab the phone book and search hurriedly for phone numbers. Can you trust this girl or that girl? Will the kids be miserable or cry if you leave them? These are legitimate questions deserving of your time, so take your time to feel comfortable about your babysitting plans and try to plan for those much needed moments of peace in advance before you reach the desperate stage. This will help to ensure you that your time away is really the peace you so need.

# LINE UP THE BABYSITTERS

"Mom, I'm bored," you hear one of them whine. You bite your lip and think of all the entertaining you have done. You dial the phone quickly before you lose your nerve.

"Sorry, darling, but mommy is going to take a few hours off."

Mass shock hits your household. All eyes and ears turn towards you. An amazing transition takes place that may manifest itself in a variety of ways. Your 2-4 feet little creatures make a miraculous change and instantly become your parents. They ask, either in their most pathetic quiet guilt instilling voices or in their demanding selfish, spoiled voices, "But, where are you going? How long will you be gone? What are we going to do? Are you going to get us something?"

Your infant begins to cry pitifully, develops colic or a fever. Your toddler falls and bumps his head as you're getting dressed and your preschooler clutches and clings to your legs and has to be physically pried from you. Early elementary grade children may actually enjoy the babysitter, depending on who it is and they may be very pronounced with their dislikes and likes. They may actually be so ecstatic that you're leaving that you wonder if they think you are really being as bad as you think you are. Adolescents will want you first to make sure they have their own exciting plans or they may welcome the opportunity to cradle the telephone for the afternoon.

Finally the plans are set. You pick up the sitter, give her or him an hour of instructions and a quick CPR course. Then you climb into the car, plug in your tape, and try not to look back at the angelic faces (the same ones that were screaming earlier), to see if those were really tears dripping off their faces or just another ploy to push your guilt button. You try to erase your mind and switch gears from motherhood to personhood before you leave the driveway. Okay, it's hard to do. In reality it usually takes anywhere from 1–3 hours to 3 days depending on the stress level you have reached. Unfortunately, by that time it's usually time to come home. But at least you tried!

Where should you go and what should you do? The possibilities are endless. A nice long drive, lunch with a friend, shopping, a few hours at the park to read a good book, a movie, a day at the beauty salon, aerobics; basically. Anything that is pleasurable to you and helps you to relax. You'll be amazed at the difference in your attitude, your ability to cope with the minor irritations that were beginning to pile up, and your love for your children and yourself will be revived.

But, beware that you don't fall into the babysitter trap. Several possibilities lie in this trap. If your babysitter is young enough to play with your children, which children love, then your house will probably look like a village destroyed by a sudden earthquake when you return. Unfortunately this is sometimes grounds for vowing that going out really isn't worth it, but don't believe that. Suck up your anger, try to remember the last few pleasurable hours, and start the overhaul. Then another trap: you finally thought you had grown up and left your parents and now have no one to answer to. Wrong! Now it's worse. There's not only your own children, but there is the babysitter, her parents, and your parents (if they happen to call while you're out, they will undoubtedly tell you that the babysitter is too young and irresponsible and they can't believe you left your child with this other child, that they never went out and left you). And last, unfortunately by the time you get a good babysitter trained, he or she has grown into a teenager who is too busy dating or has another part time job. Then you have to start all over.

Is it worth it, you ask. CERTAINLY! YOU ARE WORTH IT! YES! YES! YES! SAVE YOUR SANITY!

Your children will enjoy you more if you are happy. When you love yourself, your children will love you more and learn to love themselves more. When you respect and take time for yourself, your children learn to respect you and the time you need.

So, keep the phone book handy and LINE UP THE BABY-SITTERS!

Don't let the babysitting trap get you. Follow these simple tips to make the whole experience go a little smoother and refill your fuel tank as often as needed.

## TIPS

- Set a special time for yourself. The kids will learn to expect it and you will learn to relax a little faster

- Choose your sitter carefully. Use your instincts. If you don't like or feel comfortable with someone, your child probably won't, so look for someone you trust

- Try to use sitters consistently so your children and the sitter are comfortable with each other (especially for younger ones)

- Always leave emergency numbers, neighbor's numbers, work numbers, and a number where you can be reached, etc.

- Leave simple meals so the sitter doesn't have to use the oven

- Have a list of household and family rules posted. This makes it easier if your child tries to coax the sitter into letting him or her do something inappropriate

- Give simple rules and instructions to your children and the sitter, preferably together so both know what you mean

- Be flexible but set realistic rules about bedtime

- Set up reward system for your child for following rules with babysitter

- Try not to call. Leave a number for the sitter to call you

- Don't allow babysitters to have friends of the opposite sex over while they are sitting for you

- Remind the sitter to watch young ones carefully, also not to give any kind of medicine without talking to you first

- Ask the sitter and your child to help clean up. Let them know your expectations from the start

- Make a babysitter box; fill with special games, stickers, workbooks, toys, puzzles (anything you think your child might enjoy)

- Make a list of favorite games, songs, and stories your child likes

- Leave an art or craft project for the sitter and child to complete

- Suggest they make a picnic, enjoy, and clean up

- Rent a movie and leave a special snack

- Encourage the sitter to play with the child, encourage them to clean up, make clean up a game, assign jobs

- Suggest the sitter make a list of good behaviors the child does; be specific

- Think and act positive about the whole experience. It will rub off on your kids

- Then have a good time! Getting a satisfying babysitter requires work and time, but you'll be glad you did it. You'll be amazed at how a few outings for yourself can rejuvenate you and your loving attitude.

# PACK 'EM UP AND SHIP 'EM OFF: CAMPS

"It's off to camp we go,
It's off to camp we go,
Heigh ho, oh, mother dear,
It's off to camp we go."

"It's off to camp you go,
It's off to camp you go,
Hip Hip Hooray, my kids,
It's off to camp you go."

You may have voted out the family camping trip this year and opted for another kind of camp experience.

Pack 'em up and ship 'em off, camps, is it really for your child or for your sanity?

Correct answer: possibly both, if you choose wisely.

You may have dreamed of going to a camp when you were little and even drawn pictures and made up stories about your camp experiences to share on the first day of school but were never given the opportunity to actually attend one. Or you may sit on the other end of the spectrum and, as a child, you were practically mailed to camp on day one of summer with no return address and claimed only on the last day of parcel pick up. You might have envied all the stories of fun days at camp from the other kids or you may have nightmares of homesick evenings in a hot dirty cabin with mosquitoes thriving on you for their dinner.

Camp can be a fun and rewarding experience for both you and your child if you take the time to think through and choose the right camp. Whether you are a working parent and need child care for the summer or an at home parent needing a semi structured week or two of activities for your child to break up the monotony of home life, camps abound for your pleasure.

*Important considerations when choosing a camp:*

> Age and maturity of your child, cost of camp, length of camp (day, half day, overnight, one week, two), type of camp, activities planned and appropriateness for your child, location of camp and distance from home, transportation, supervision, visitation, food, safety precautions and emergency care procedures, etc.

*Where to find a camp:*

> Day care centers offer summer camp programs both for children in the program and parents needing summer care. Activities usually include swimming (sometimes lessons are included) and local field trips such as roller skating, movies, visits to local parks, etc. Prices vary with each facility so shop around for the best deal. Some churches offer similar summer programs.

A variety of day or half day camps are usually offered through local recreation and parks departments, arts centers, local museums, schools, gymnastic and dance centers, sports centers, nature centers, the YWCA and YMCA, Girl Scout and Boy Scouts, etc. Check newspapers, local magazines, bookstores and libraries for listings of activities offered in your area.

If you are really industrious, can't afford or just don't want to pay for an away from home camp or have young children not ready for that experience, set up a week or two of camp at home. Plan special activities that week and call it camp. Make name tags, set up a schedule with arts and crafts activities, drama activities, music, special snacks, field trips, special outside activities, etc. You may want to include the neighbor's kids for a small fee or suggest the idea with other neighbors and form a trade off for camps at their house. Your children will enjoy planning the activities for their camp as much as the activities themselves.

*Types of camps offered:*

Sports camps; baseball, soccer, basketball, hockey, tennis, swim (any sport imaginable); some local through recreation and parks and overnight camps offered through Swim Clubs, Baseball Associations, colleges, etc. Gymnastic camps offered through Gymnastics Centers, dance camps at dance centers, art camps at arts centers, etc.

*Age and maturity of your child:*

Obviously infants and toddlers are not ready for camps. One option is a mother's morning out program in a loving church setting or home setting. If your child is in a stable child care situation due to your work and camp type activities are planned within their normal child care setting then he may handle it fine. Pre-schoolers do well at half day camps offered through churches, an art camp or a sports camp of their interest. Overnight camps are best for older children, preferably age nine and up. Even thirteen year olds usually say the first week of camp is fun, but the second is long and they are ready to come home. For children not ready to spend a long time away from home, day camps (9:00-3:00) are good, because the child is active during the day but can still come home in the evenings.

*Preparing for Camp:*

Mothers, remember that even in labor, you didn't panic or get upset as long as you knew what was going to happen. Preparing you for all the steps of childbirth eased your mind and let you relax and enjoy (?) the experience. Your child's reaction and enjoyment of camp will be enhanced by your attitude and preparation. Prepare your child both physically and mentally for camp. Make sure he gets lots of rest ahead of time (he'll need it since camps are usually physically exhausting), and by packing appropriately. Be sure to obtain a suggested packing list for the trip if it's overnight, so you can include all the necessaries. Find out the schedule of activities, rules, visitation, hours, expectations, meal plans, etc., and discuss with your child ahead of time. Pack proper clothing, extra spending money, stationery (for overnight camps), a book with the days marked or perhaps a journal to record thoughts in each day. (This also allows him to gage his time and how long he is there, how much longer until he's home.)

Be positive and emphasize the "fun" he or she will have. If your child expresses reservations, discuss these feelings and help him deal with them. Talk about what he can do if he feels sad or misses you. Suggest he think of a particular silly thing or experience you shared or if he's sad draw you a picture or a postcard about something funny at camp. If your child is at an overnight camp, be careful when you telephone. Let your child know you're glad he's having fun. Don't whine about how much you miss him (if you do), and don't sound sad yourself. Children pick up on the tones of our voices and react so try to be as positive as possible.

Then, moms enjoy the time your child is at camp. Do all those things you want to do for yourself and don't feel guilty! You deserve it.

So, pack 'em up and ship 'em off; camps; one way to survive the summer!

## TO VACATION OR TO A REST HOME

The walls around you seem to be caving in like the blueberries that get hidden by the mix. Even the pool has become routine. You've exhausted all your ideas for entertainment and your body aches for a different air and wide open spaces.

Vacation! At last. The one week of the year you plan to relax, forget the laundry, eat junk food, and get away from it all. Perhaps your dream is a cabin in the mountains or a tour of half the country. Whatever your idea of vacation is, you've saved for it, planned for it, and you need it desperately.

The reservations are made. You have new tires on the van. The suitcases are stuffed. You have a half dozen bottles of assorted sun screens. The pets are taken care of, and you have two weeks of work done ahead of time at the (paying) job just to allow you the peace of no phone calls. You stand before the car or van in dismay. You're speechless as you watch your kids drag armloads of stuffed animals and games into the back seat, pushing and arguing over where each one will sit.

"Kids, we're only going to be gone a week," you hear your husband say.

"But, Daddy, I can't leave Blue Bear behind. He'll get lonely."

"And you know we need the Nintendo. What'll we do if it rains one day?"

You and your husband shake your heads in defeat and you bend to hold the mass of suitcases, toys, groceries, coolers, beach chairs, etc., in the back as he attempts to shut the back hatch.

"Nobody opens it til we get there!" the father orders as he slams it shut.

Ten miles down the road you hear, "How much longer til we get there, Dad?"

"Mommy, I got to go to the bathroom."

"He hit me."

Yes, you've started your vacation. Restful, not yet, but you still have hopes.

"Mommy, I don't feel good," one of the children cries.

You ignore the first five whines, then turn to see. Potty training falls to the pits as the unexpected, the unwanted, the unbelievable explosion occurs. Common diarrhea has just struck your youngest. Your six hour trip turns into ten as you get the opportunity to tour every restroom for four hundred miles. You wrestle with your recently potty trained two year old that it is okay to wear a diaper, just for the trip. "NO!" he refuses. "I'm a big boy now."

Each time you climb back into the car you hear, "I"m not sitting by him, not me. Are we almost there yet? How many more hours?"

"Kids, this is our vacation. This is supposed to be fun," you remind them.

You learned early in your life with children that with any more than two children, at least one is unhappy at all times. Reciting this revelation temporarily helps you cope.

"Where is that garbage bag?" you mutter as you search under the seat, you're sure you put one in (always prepared for anything).

"Oh, I think it's in the suitcase," you say turning to your husband.

"NO WAY, I'm not opening the back," he declares. "Just throw the dirty clothes away! We'll buy some more."

He starts the engine and you're off for your final hour of travel. Once you start crossing the bridges, the children get excited and you begin to hear the beach calling your name. (Not Mommy, your real name, the one you had before children). You pull in the driveway to your home for the next few days and the children pile out, racing for the beach.

"Wait a minute," you yell, "you guys have to help, you know."

You begin to set the rules; no going to the beach without a grown-up, no going out very far, etc., etc.

Your restful vacation begins with early mornings. Young kids feel compelled to rise with the sun and be on the beach by 8:00.

You end the days with late bedtimes because you understand that everyone is too excited to sleep.

It takes you thirty minutes to haul things down to the beach and fifteen to coat everyone in sun screen. By the time you get comfortable in your chair with your magazine someone is hungry or thirsty.

"We just ate," you plead. "Mommy just wants to sit for a few minutes. Now you go play. See those other children making a sand castle."

"Play with me, Mommy. Come help me find shells."

"I'm hot."

"Aaaah. ... a jelly fish stung me."

Someone cries, "I've got sand in my eyes."

You jump to the call like a mother tiger in the wild, tossing the magazine in your seat and racing to the rescue. Clean the eyes, fix another meal, hang the wet towels up, sweep the sand out of the kitchen, STOP! Your vision of hours of lying in the lounge chair sipping a drink, reading mindless novels, and sunbathing sailed out with the first tide.

The second day you don't even bother to drag the chairs down since you quickly discovered that "if found, mothers sitting restfully on the beach would be fined."

About the third day you all settle into a routine and things become a little more restful. You explore different activities with the kids. You find the bike rental and go riding. You find the pool, the t-shirt shop, and a MacDonald's with a playground. Dad has taken sufficient pictures and videos for the trip and you and he may even steal a few quiet moments together while the children rest inside.

The fifth morning your illusions shatter when you hear one of your children groan, "I'm bored."

"How can anyone be bored at the beach?" you wonder. The "I never got to go to the beach when I was a kid, and I would have given anything to have, you're so lucky," speech fights with your tongue.

You look at the sunburned face of your baby and wonder why the sunscreen didn't work and you have to scrub the sand from the tub because you can't stand it any longer.

Everyone is tired on the morning you plan to leave and begs, "can't we just stay one more day. Please, please, please, I'll be your best friend."

You chuckle, trying to console yourself and then reply, "It looks overcast today anyway, like it might rain." Your weary family rests and talk and are fairly calm on the ride home for the first couple of hours.

Then it begins again, "How much longer? Are we almost there?"

The last hour turns into eternity's dragon and you find yourself doling out candy for every quiet 10 minute period like animal trainers do to their beasts.

Heavy sighs echo as you finally pull into your own driveway. You need a vacation now, you think, just to rest. As you begin to unload the masses (it looks like you brought home more than you took), the children make a dive for the TV. You turn to your husband and begin planning the next vacation.

"How about two years?" you ask.

"Five. No sooner than five," he says.

"Deal" you shake hands on it, "next year I'm going to a rest home."

## TIPS TO IMPROVE YOUR VACATION

- Once again, set realistic expectations. Fight the misbelief that children miraculously become angelic creatures who do not fight, whine, or cry just because you are on vacation. Although we all want our children to appreciate and thank us profusely for all that we do for them, don't be crushed if they don't. In fact, after a few years of parenting, you'll probably suffer a heart attack if they do.

- Children are egocentrical by their nature and at some point in the future hopefully some miracle or shaking of their brains will make them realize our sacrifices, but it will probably not be until they have experienced natural childbirth and lived with their own children. Tactful reminders of manners can train them somewhat, but lectures only create anger and a battle of the wills.

- Plan in advance. Check with the hotel, cabin, campground, etc., and find out what they provide and what things you need to bring; for example, how many beds, if you need to bring linens, if a kitchen is included, porta cribs, etc.

- Try to rent a house or condo with a kitchen. Take along quick breakfast meals like cereal, doughnuts, etc., and snacks for late night or after rest times. If staying in a hotel, request adjoining rooms.

- Remember, no one sleeps as well away from home. Avoid caffeine for you and your child in the evenings. Give yourself a little extra time for settling down. Keep to a routine, bath, story time, water, and bathroom. A familiar toy or blanket, lullaby tape or soft music can also comfort and help relax a child.

- Make sure your child is well before you get in the car. If any doubts, see your Dr. Always take pediatrician's number with you on vacation in case of emergency.

- If your child has a medical problem (for example, diabetes, seizures, allergies), find out where the nearest hospital is to your vacation spot. Have all information available by the phone in case you need it in an emergency.

- Take a first aid box (you can make one from an old lunch box). Include band aids, first aid creme, Benadryl (for bug bites),

Tylenol, a thermometer, cleaning swabs, gauge, cough medicine, ear drops, Icecap, antibiotic cream and tape. What you think won't happen, just may. Be prepared. With children, anything is possible.

- For babies and young children take wipes, changing pad, stroller, porta bed, portable high chair (attachable to table), change of clothes (accessible in car), bag for dirty clothes or diapers, bottles and baby food prepared ahead of time.

- Try to vacation during less busy times for area. Also plan for the weather. For example, avoid places like Disney World during the hottest weeks of the summer.

- At the beach, rent or take covered chairs or a tarp. Children love to play under this and it protects them from too much sun. Young children will want to be at the beach before breakfast and back by lunch. Let them rest inside after lunch. This again gives them a break from the sun. Use lots of sunscreen. Feed them breakfast before you go to the beach. Then take a thermos of water and snacks to the beach with you or the kids will be begging to come back up for lunch before you have everyone coated in sunscreen and you'll be begging to go home.

- Label all your beach, pool and sand toys with permanent markers for less confusion when other children want to share and mistake ownership.

- Beach games like paddle ball, volleyball, frisbee, etc., are great entertainers. Play coke ball: set up like a baseball game, use a plastic bat and ball. At each base, person has to stop and take a sip of coke before going on to the next base.

- At the beach (or any place you go), explore textures, sights, and sounds by making a game of it. Name the different sounds you hear. Draw the sights. Feel and describe the things you collect. At the beach, dig for sand crabs. Make footprints or shapes in the sand with your feet, hands, etc. Make roads, tunnels, castles, animals and other sand sculptures. Play race the waves. Draw or write in the sand with sticks or your finger. Bring a magnifying glass to explore with. Collect driftwood, shells, etc., that have floated in. Keep a journal of the things you find. Make nature or shell collages. String shells to make jewelry.

- For camping trips and beach trips pack lots of extra clothes. Look for places with laundry facilities. When camping, take plastic to cover things, tarp for food area, easy and pre-prepared foods.

- Take plenty of garbage bags for wet and dirty things. On the first day of vacation designate a box, basket or bag for dirty clothes. Insist the children use it. Hang wet beach towels out over rail (if you have one) for the sun to dry and cut down on your laundry. Take a mesh net bag to put wet toys in to drain.

- For ski trips or vacations in cooler spots, take lots of clothes for layering, plenty of socks, mittens, vaseline for chapped lips, cheeks, and hands, lotions for dry and wind burned skin.

- Bug repellent is a necessity for almost any type vacation.

- Take plastic containers for snacks. (Older children can handle plastic bags, but they are not recommended for young children.)

- Remember comfortable clothes and shoes! And mothers, always keep a purse full of bandaids for blisters and boo boos!

- Investigate nearby restaurants and other attractions in the area before hand. Save the candlelit romantic spots for you and your spouse. Look for family restaurants. Teach manners at home first. You can't expect kids to become angels in public if they haven't had preparation. Keep crayons and a small pad of paper in your purse, too, for those waiting times at restaurants. (Yes, mothers, you may have guessed by now, you need a big purse!)

Little games like "I Spy," word games, listening for rhyming words, and counting objects in the room can entertain preschool and school age children. When waiting for food, entertain your children with stories; stories about yourself when you were little, stories about each of them, other family members like grandmas and grandpas, etc.

- Don't expect to have quiet relaxing meals. Babies always want to nurse at meal times and toddlers want to toddle. Parents can toss a coin or take turns feeding, walking, and exercising little ones while waiting for food. There will once again be a time when Mom and Dad actually sit and eat at the same time again. See; "Where Have All the Flowers Gone."

- On airplanes, take small snacks with you. Often times children won't eat the food served in hotels, airplanes, etc. Some airlines will prepare special children's meals of hamburgers or hotdogs if you request 24 hours in advance.

- Schedule flights, sightseeing and visits to attractions in early mornings, after rest times, etc. If possible, buy tickets in advance to avoid long lines. Plan for bathroom breaks, snacks, rest times, etc. Take a back pack with small snacks and water bottle for times when you are hiking or touring and can't find a drink machine or snack place. Think of interests of ages of your children and plan accordingly. Long trips to museums are better planned for older children, parks and recreational areas are a must for younger ones.

- Although, you love spontaneity, your children may not be so flexible. Over tired, over due for meals, and over heated children make very unlovable children.

- If visiting parks or museums, check ahead for times for programs and shows. If you have a child with special needs, always check in advance to see if special provisions can be made for you.

- Take appropriate clothing. Lightweight jackets are needed even on the beach at night. Sun screen, sun hats, after sun lotion, a blanket in the car for emergency, umbrellas are all necessities.

- When packing give children a list and a limit of items to bring depending on the child's age: for example, two stuffed toys, two games, etc.

- Have children bring their own money (they've earned) for souvenirs and momentos of the trip. (Concentrate on children earning this a few weeks before your trip.)

- Plan a bag of activities and snacks for the ride (see "Are We There Yet?")

- Plan simple easy to fix meals to keep you out of the kitchen. Children will remember the crabbing and softball game on the beach, not the five course dinner, meat, two vegetables, two fruits, and the linen napkins.

- Try to be flexible and more relaxed with schedules but don't stray too far or you'll regret it. Overtired kids breed trouble even at the most exciting of attractions. Routines for younger children are important.

- For older children you may want to include a friend, give a little extra freedom (within limits), and talk to and try to respect their wants.

- Teach your child a little about photography before or on your trip. If possible, allow him his own camera and film.

- Consider different kinds of vacations; amusements parks, beaches, the mountains, camping, resorts, skiing, fishing, a wild west tour. You may want to make several mini vacations if you can't afford a week or two away. Visit local parks and recreational areas within your area such as water parks, storytelling festivals, museums, lakes, etc.

- If possible, take a babysitter (or your older child, if of age), can babysit and let you and your spouse enjoy a couple of evenings out.

- Club Med offers vacations with activities for children and free time for parents although prices vary and may be costly, but if you want to splurge check into their different programs.

- Vacationing with another family can lower your costs, provide your child or children with playmates, give adults a break during the trip, and be fun. Be sure to consider carefully the family you go with, parenting styles, compatibility of children, activities available, accommodations, etc., before you undertake this, but with careful planning this can be a fun trip for all.

- Realize your idea of vacation and fun may differ from your child's and each child's view may also differ, especially at different ages. Discuss this in advance and plan for everyone. Tell them your expectations and try to teach them to respect each other's choices, likes and dislikes instead of criticizing one person for being different.

- Then relax, enjoy, and be a kid yourself. Someday your children will refuse to be seen with you in public, much less go on vacation with you and you will pour over the photo albums, weeping at all the memories of trips taken together, the hikes and the long car trips, you and your child cuddled together taking an afternoon nap in the hammock, the baby sea turtles you discovered, all the precious moments you shared. The trivial upsets like the time one of the kids put a popcorn seed in his ear and you had to go to the emergency room on the way to the beach or the time your daughter named all the worms you bought for fishing and hid them in her jacket pocket where they escaped in the middle of the restaurant will bring you laughter and, yes, you may even find yourself yearning to make sandcastles but think you look too ridiculous to do so without a child to use as an excuse.

# CHAPTER 7
## WORDS OF WISDOM

"The early bird catches the worm," but I'm not a morning person you think.

"Sticks and stones can break my bones but words can never hurt me." True or False.

"I would have rather have had a spanking than a "Talking to" as my father used to say."

Words, words, only words?

Things you vowed you would never say or do as a parent but may already have, DO THESE WORDS SOUND FAMILIAR?

*I will never say:*

"Do you want a spanking?"

"Believe me, honey, this hurts me more than it does you."

"Do you want me to give you something to cry about."

"I will give you to the count of 3 - 1...2...3..."

"You have to eat every bite on your plate. Do you know the children in Africa would love to have that food. They're starving to death."

"You'll understand when you grow up."

"Because I'm the Mom, that's why!"

"Don't you ever ever do that again. Do you understand me, boy?"

"Where's your brain? You'd lose your head if it wasn't attached."

"We'll see."

*Things You Wish Your Mom Had Said Instead:*

IF YOU WANT TO HAVE CHILDREN YOU MUST:

Enjoy picking up after other people and do it cheerfully.

Require no privacy or time alone, especially in the bathroom.

Have an iron stomach, enjoy the smell of soured milk and smeared baby food, enjoy being a short order cook and eating in shifts.

You must like lots of noise, especially at the dinner table and never want to eat alone again with your spouse.

Require very little sleep and love being awakened at all hours of the night, having extra bodies crawling in your bed at any time.

Have dreamed of driving a taxi cab service when you were little. You like big cars or vans, not small sports cars.

Love to stand in lines and have a strong back (to hold your tired whiny children when you're waiting for two hours to see Santa Claus or the Easter Bunny). You also enjoy staying up late at night putting together small pieces of toys with directions that are written only in a foreign language.

Like to ride wild rides at amusement parks, enjoy screaming, and spending large sums of money to win prizes.

Enjoy putting toys together and fixing broken ones.

Like to roller skate with a hundred children and loud music playing in the background.

Enjoy studying, doing projects, and relearning Algebra two or three times (with each child).

Be able to make a costume at an evening's notice.

Enjoy doing laundry, scrubbing toilets, cleaning dishes, grocery shopping, mopping the kitchen, clipping coupons, untying knots from dirty tennis shoes, and trying to discover a successful way to keep the toothpaste off the sink, mirror, floor and bathroom cabinets.

Love lizards, frogs, turtles, gerbils, and all other kinds of pet (pests included).

Words of Wisdom, Words of Warning or Words of Experience?

Parents, choose your words carefully. Remember the three most important words you can say to your child: I LOVE YOU! Say them daily.

*DO*

Teach by telling and modeling the use of words instead of physical methods to express feelings and emotions, including the range from love to anger. Allow your child to express negative feelings with words. Do draw boundaries and stress that even words have limits. (For ex.; you may not allow your child to curse you or degrade you.) Also by discussing problems you and your child can learn problem solving techniques which will be valuable to him or her later in life. If a pattern of negative words becomes dominant, work to change this. A child can express dislike or anger about something, but not be allowed to continue to focus on that feeling or incident for an extended period of time. To remain healthy and happy he or she must learn to let go of feelings and focus on more positive things that have happened.

Positive words from you can encourage positive behavior from your child. Be realistic in your praise (children know when you are not, for ex.; you can't tell your child he is the best player on the team if he obviously isn't, but you can help him to point out and emphasize the specific things he did well). Everyone likes to be praised and thanked, so your words of respect and praise will get you further than put downs or scowls.

Then the next time you hear these words, "Mom, what are we going to do today?," turn to your child and say, "Let's hear it from you!" Then listen to his words!

# LET'S HEAR IT FROM THE KIDS

"YEAH! School's out. No more homework! We can lie on the couch and watch TV; stay up as late as we want, go to the pool all day, go see movies, play with our friends, goof off. No one to tell us what to do."

"Hey, kids, you need to go make your bed up and I need some help folding the laundry."

"MOM! It's summer. You expect us to work. We've worked in school all year! Summer is suppose to be fun."

You blink your eyes trying to remember if your children have seen a movie entitled, "Mom, the Fun Slave" lately. An attitude adjustment is definitely in order and before your temper grips you by the claws, your vampire blood sizzles, and you attack, stop and have that chat with your children that you may have forgotten to have. Remember; listen to your kids, let them share their ideas about their expectations and wants for the summer. You share yours and then you together with your children can make a plan.

Children do feel stress from school. Children who are involved in extra curricular activities feel double stressed at times and you do need to accept that children do need a rest from school work and the pressures of other activities. However, work around the house is the neverending story. So, definitely cut down on the "rush hours" of busy schedules. However, if in English 101 your child failed to learn that the synonym for "Mom" is not "Children's Fun Slave," then now is the time to teach it at home.

## The Children Speak:

*This summer I want to:*

play games

go to water parks

swim

go camping

go to big amusement parks

party

anything but work

go to the beach

go fishing

make money

go on vacation

meet girls

meet boys

ride bikes

read

paint

play with my friends

sleep late

stay up late

hang out with my friends

swim team

go to the mall

get a summer job

babysit

do art projects

play putt putt

watch tv

go to movies

learn to sew

learn to ski

have picnics

go to the lake

go hiking

travel

stay on a houseboat

relax and be lazy

get a motorcycle

play in the sprinkler

play outside

play hopscotch, jump rope, hide and seek

Play 1-2-3 redlight and May I

*study for college (?); did someone really say that?*

have my parents go away and let me stay alone so I could do whatever I want

# PARENT ALERT

Although asking the children what they want to do is helpful, as parents we have to realize that what children want and what is best for them is not always the same. It isn't certain why but some children can entertain themselves from the moment they are born and the mystery of the ones who need constant guidance from minute to minute is both perplexing and frustrating. Rather than trying to constantly entertain your child, try to train him to "think" for himself. This will be a valuable gift and tool for him the rest of his life. Expect and demand that he entertain himself for certain periods of time, then listen to his wishes and make compromises between his demands and your ideas from your parenting perspective. You can't leave (even a teenager) for an entire summer without any supervision, but you can leave him for shorter times to care for himself. Ease into responsibility. Financially you can't take your child to a movie one day, skating the next, putt putt the next, an amusement park the next, etc. Children must learn the boundaries of money and also that life isn't just one big whirlwind of excitement. Setting up limits for "entertainment" and allowing children to make choices within these limits teaches responsibility, makes them feel more in control and takes the heat off of you which in turn makes every day life a little smoother.

So, before your purse is empty and you scream, "Calgon, take me away!" listen to your kids, then talk, set up limits, choices, compromises, and perhaps you and your child will both enjoy your summer.

# EARTH SHATTERING REVELATIONS FROM MOMS

"Just a spoonful of sugar helps the medicine go down, the medicine go down, the medicine go down. Just a spoonful of sugar helps the medicine go down, in the most delightful way." Earthshattering, hardly, but sometimes we forget the most natural and practical advice is the best.

Try to start each day with a smile and a positive attitude. A dose of love, a hug a kiss, an "I love you" can help smooth any day and start you all off on a better foot.

Establish from the beginning that you are not the entertainer. Your job as Mom is to help coordinate activities, guide them in decision making and activities and act as a support person. Put the responsibility on the children to entertain themselves for certain periods of time. Provide a balance between Mom entertainment activities and "self directed entertainment activities."

Encourage children to make lists of activities or suggestions, needs, etc., so you can discuss this and plan for different things.

If your family seems to fall apart without structure during the summer, set a simple schedule or routine for your day at home. Plan the day before. Let the children help in planning and organizing the day or week in advance so they know what to expect, what to look forward to, and when to work in their chores. Set up a weekly calendar and pencil in activities.

Assign chores, even small daily ones, so you don't feel like you're doing all the work and they're having all the fun. They may argue that it's their vacation, but it's yours, too. Everyone feels better and gets along better when they are an active part of the group. Also, requiring your children to clean up after themselves and their friends on a daily basis will prevent you from exploding when you discover the crushed Doritos and chocolate chip cookies on the basement floor a week later and the ants that have already invaded your house for their indoor picnic.

Organize your house from the beginning. Establish a shoe box or shelf near the door for depositing shoes when children enter the house (you know they'll never make it to the shoe bin in their rooms). Set up a place for wet bathing suits and towels. Use hooks or shelves low enough for children to reach. Dirty clothes hampers (small baskets) in each room help. Organize toys and limit spaces where they may be. In the den, make a basket or shelf for crayons, paper, books, puzzles, games that children can do while they watch TV (you might turn this time into something productive after all). Other toys should be kept in their rooms or playroom. Prepare shelves and baskets or boxes in garage or laundry room for outside toys like bats, balls, skates, etc.

Try to limit food and drinks to the kitchen for clean up. You may want to make snacks in the den a special treat. When you do allow food in the den, use a picnic cloth or tray and stress that it be used (helps contain the mess to one area and easier clean up, also keeps those delightful crumbs from underneath the sofa cushion).

Limit phone times.

Set up a chart with check and reward system for completed chores.

Suggested chores: clean bathrooms, wash low windows, help wash car, empty trash, bring trash cans up to house, help plant flowers, weed yard or garden, water flowers, wash dishes, set table, pick up toys, stack newspapers for recycling, clean garage, sweep garage and patio, fold laundry, mow yard, care for pets, etc. Make a chore chart and either assign certain chores to certain children (depending on age) or let children choose certain number of chores. Give a time limit (sometime within the next century will not do) and have a system for keeping track. Young children may need a simple chart. For example, on paper posted on refrigerator write: Chore Chart: empty trash 50 cents, fold laundry 75 cents, sweep 30 cents, etc.

Older children may want to make a flyer for neighbors and list odd jobs, then circulate to earn extra money. Jobs suggested: babysit, clean yards, pull weeds, pet sit, sweep driveways and patios, wash cars, mow yards.

Set up a special account, "Fun Money" account for movies, amusement parks, miniature golf, etc. Work this in according to your budget and discuss this with the children. Place a limit according to your finances and teach your children to make choices within those limits. Also, set up a method for earning allowance or fun money so your child can have his own spending money. This enables him to learn responsibility, make choices about spending, set priorities, and to see what happens when the pocketbook is empty. The concept that you actually have to put money into the bank, that those nice people with the jar of suckers don't just give it to you, is not knowledge your child was born with.

Later bedtimes become normal but try not to stray too far from the norm or you and your child both suffer.

Do your homework: Research newspapers and magazines for listings of community activities which might be of interest. Check the entertainment section of the paper for art festivals, plays, puppet shows, museums, etc. Local bookstores sometimes have available magazines or books with listings of interest areas in the city, community, and neighboring towns where you live.

Check local nature centers, libraries, zoos, etc., for summer programs and events offered. Special classes, programs, and camps are offered through local art centers, Parks and Recreation Dept., nature centers, YMCA's and YWCA's, churches and community schools, usually for reasonable prices. Local libraries usually offer special story hours for young children. Churches offer Bible schools and youth groups for older children which sometimes have weekly activities planned for the summer.

Call local farms, news stations, and large companies which might allow groups of children to visit. Organize a group of neighborhood kids and moms and take a field trip together.

Try a new sport for you, your child, or both; learn horseback riding, scuba diving, swimming, etc.

Ask your church for names of families or members that might need help over the summer, such as food, chores or odd jobs around the house, transportation. You and your family can make this a worthwhile learning project and help out someone else at the same time.

Visit nursing homes or hospitals and offer story times and visits with patients.

Summer is a great time for a new pet if your family is in the market. Be sure to discuss and delegate responsibilities before adopting or buying the pet.

Form a co-op with neighbors or friends for trading off children, play groups, or carpools for outings.

Back to nature; take nature walks at home, parks, etc., and make collections of rocks, leaves, etc., to study. Visit the library and check out books to investigate your collections.

Children love crafts so choose one or some of your favorites or theirs and have fun. Sewing, needlepoint, building, putting together model cars, painting, weaving, making jewelry, and countless other simple hobby projects and supplies are available at craft stores.

Sidewalk chalks lends to hours of creativity and games, then washes off with the rain.

Plan a bike parade; let children decorate bikes and parade.

The "VooDoo Tube" and Nintendo disease: to be or not to be? TV and video games are a part of our lives. However, refrain from using them solely to babysit your kids. Limit TV and video time. Discuss this with children. Give them a time limit per day. Let them choose programs they want to watch within limits and appropriateness. Encourage shows on the educational channel. Discuss programs with your child; reality vs. fantasy, morals, etc.

Plant a garden. Let children help. Learn about different kinds of seeds, vegetables, flowers, etc. Children can help plant, water, and take care of the garden.

Let children set up small businesses: Lemonade Stand, Tomato stand, etc. They'll have fun setting up the business. They can make posters to advertise, set prices, learn about cost and profits.

Read, read, read. With young children, read to them. Older children will enjoy reading to themselves. Visit the library and let both groups choose their own books. You may want to provide art supplies and let them do follow up art about their favorite books. Let your child keep a summer reading list with rewards for certain goals met.

Bookstores, gift and card shops, and specialty shops offer books for children with activity suggestions. Your child's teacher or the school counselor may also have a monthly calendar for each month of the summer with suggestions.

For young children, sand and water play are favorites. Sand boxes and small swimming pools provide hours of entertainment as well as learning experiences. Provide different size containers, as well as toy trucks, animals, etc., for the children to measure, explore, and use their imagination.

Have a family game hour where everyone plays board games or cards. Pop popcorn and have it as a special event.

Prepare a program or show for the neighbors' kids or friends. Make your costumes, practice, and have a show time. Your children will enjoy making invitations, posters to advertise, and setting up for the program.

Name a certain night of the week "Mexican" night or "Japanese" night, and prepare foods from that country. Children can help cook and may even want to set the table up as a restaurant. One child or parent might be the waitress or waiter.

Let your child help you cook. Letting them help you measure, count, pour, etc., is a learning experience as well as one children enjoy.

Let each child plan a menu for the week, go to the store with you and select and find all the ingredients, then help prepare.

Pre teens and teens can hold part time jobs, from babysitting to the grocery store to the mall, depending on the age and requirements of the job. This not only provides them with the spending money they want but teaches them responsibility and keeps them out of trouble.

Look for organized sports in your area that your child may be interested in. Also day camps for different sports are offered at sports centers, gymnastic and dance centers, parks and community schools, YMCA's and YWCA's.

Plan shopping outings. Take extra bottles or crackers for babies and take snacks with you for infants and toddlers. Shop at times when stores are least crowded, usually in morning. Young children often do better in mornings and you can make it home for an afternoon rest. Go shopping with only one or two goals in mind. For example, purchase film for camera, socks for kids, eat lunch, visit pet store. Keep the interest level and age of your child in mind and try to arrange the activities they enjoy such as throwing pennies in the fountain, looking in the bookstore, etc. Remind your children to take their savings (spending money) with them to use if they see something they "Have to Have." Discuss in advance your rules for them purchasing certain items with their money and the items your checkbook pays for, then stick to your guns. Save shopping for yourself for your ALONE trips. Attempting to try on ten outfits while your baby crawls out of the stroller, your toddler makes the rounds of all the dressing rooms, and your older child sits in a chair glaring at you and huffing makes a miserable day for everyone. Also, use strollers, child leashes, or hold your child's hand. Getting lost in a mall, zoo, park, or anywhere is scary for everyone and dangerous, too. Discuss with your child in advance how to handle the situation if it should ever happen. Be sure your child knows his name, phone number, and address.

Use the grocery store as a field trip. Take a trip and talk about the different kinds of fruits, vegetables, cheeses, etc. Point out unusual products and where they came from. Give child a list or certain number of items to help find. Let them compare prices.

Let your children cut out your coupons and organize them.

Decorate "me" cookies. Provide different colors of icing for eyes, nose, lips, hair.

Make button necklaces. Let your child count and sort your buttons and organize them for you.

Have your child count the number of licks it takes to get to the center of the tootsie roll pop.

Have wash day for all doll clothes. Let your child wash clothes in a large tub with soapy water, rinse and hang to dry.

# SHH! THE TEACHER IS TALKING

"Head, shoulders, knees and toes,
Head, shoulders, knees, and toes,
Head, shoulders, knees, and toes
Eyes and ears and mouth and nose
Head, shoulders, knees and toes, knees, and toes."

"Boys and girls, put your listening ears on and zip your lips. The teacher is talking. Now enjoy your summer vacation, but remember to read and use your time to learn about new places and new things. Have a great summer."

## SUGGESTIONS

• Arts, crafts, reading, trips, and camps can make your summer more fun and provide great learning experiences. Parents, spending time with your child is more valuable than all the toys you can buy. You need a balance of time for yourself and time with your child. Try to avoid using the TV as a babysitter. Take time off from your kids, but also take time to talk to, listen, and play with your kids. Set a few simple goals for you and your child at the beginning of the summer. Discuss this with your child at the beginning. Find out what each child would like to accomplish over the summer, perhaps, learn to ride a two wheel bike, take horseback riding lessons, take art lessons, learn to swim, go camping, anything is possible. Then you can plan some activities to try to meet these goals.

• Give home responsibilities and let children earn money.

• Schedule certain things but don't go overboard. Although it is an adjustment to be schedule free, it is a learning experience for children to manage their own time and entertain themselves. They need a break from the rigid schedules and busy activities of the school year.

- Use your summer to help children learn alphabet or math skills, writing, home economic skills. Try to do it in fun ways, remember a child's work is his play.

- Set up a summer reading program. Visit the library often and let your child choose books. Make a chart or list of the books your read. Examples: cut paper circles from construction paper. On each circle the child writes the name of book read, then glues them together to make a worm. See how long you can make the worm. Choose something your child is interested in; ex. dinosaurs or cars and use that as your way of recording. Cut paper cars and list books on each. You may want to give a reward for every ten books read (picture books) or three (chapter books). After reading discuss the books. Ask your child to retell the story, tell the main idea.

- Children love to sing. Song tapes, song books and fingerplay books are available for children at toy and book stores. Make up your own song, record it, and be a star musician.

- Provide lots of paper, crayons, markers, chalk, paint (your own art centers). Children can follow up stories by making pictures about the books. For example, read *Caps for Sale*, make monkey puppet or paper hats. Act out the story being the monkey or the peddler. Read *Swimmy*, then draw or paint fish and ocean scenes. Kids can also use this area as free creative art time. Set up boxes with scraps of paper, yarn, cloth, old wallpaper samples, cotton balls, dry noodles or seeds, tissue paper, etc., and let kids create on their own.

- Empty toilet paper and paper towel rolls are the beginnings of many art projects. Add materials to make rockets, butterflies, bugs, anything your imagination can think of.

- Paper plates, bags, socks, mittens, make great beginnings for puppet projects. Make a puppet character from a book you've read, an original puppet (then create your own story about the character), or a puppet animal.

- Pick a unit or subject theme (let your child choose something he or she is interested in). Visit the library and check out books on the subject. Prepare snacks or foods related to the subject, draw or do an art project about the theme. For example, dinosaurs: check out books on dinosaurs to read. Use dinosaur cookie cutters with playdough or make cookies with them. Make fossil prints by pressing toy dinosaur feet in playdough. Draw dinosaurs and paint. Make dinosaur egg by mixing soap flakes and water (thick consistency), pack around small toy dinosaur. Shape into egg shape. Let child use soap all week and as it washes away, he finds the dinosaur in the egg. Make dinosaur eggs by boiling eggs, crack the shell gently (leaving on egg), then soak eggs in KoolAid for an hour or overnight. When the child peels the egg, he sees lines of color in the egg.

- Provide hammers, small nails, and small scraps of wood. Children can design their own wood projects, then paint them. You may want to work on a birdfeeder together. Then hang and watch the birds come to eat. Talk about different kinds of birds and look for books on birds.

- Provide plastic bats, balls, badminton set, nerf balls, etc., for all kinds of out door games.

- Provide plastic rakes and shovels for little children, real ones for older kids. Children can rake straw and leaves and make playhouses or rooms out of them, design their own houses.

- Use cardboard boxes. Large ones make great playhouses, rocket ships, stores or puppet theaters. Children can spend hours just preparing and decorating the box. Smaller boxes (shoe boxes, match boxes, gift boxes, etc.) can be stacked together in various ways to make doll houses with rooms, parking garages for small cars, dioramas, a palace for bugs or storage for rock collections, etc.

- Sand and water play are always favorites for young children - middle school age. The sprinkler is a great back yard entertainer. Also provide measuring cups, spoons, different size containers (plastic, not glass), eggbeaters, funnels, shovels, etc., for children to play in sand or small water pool areas.

- Provide paint brushes and buckets of water for children to paint the house, deck, and sidewalk.

- Color different kinds of macaroni noodles with food coloring (let dry on paper towels before using). String for jewelry or glue on paper to make a collage. Kids design their own.

- Collect sea shells to sort, count, label, and use for projects. String ones with small holes for jewelry. Use in pictures or with larger shell make something out of it. For example, make a shell person or animal. Provide small seeds, buttons, string, etc., to add for making shell creation.

- Decorate or glue small shells on a pot or vase to make a shell vase. Add shells to terrarium or aquarium.

- Make an ocean in a jar. Use glass bottle or jar with lid. Fill with water and 1/2 to 3/4 full of baby oil. Add blue food coloring, shells, small plastic fish, and sand to make ocean. Then tilt the bottle sideways gently, watch the waves roll.

- Keep a sand dollar that you find. Dry it in the sun, then bleach with chlorox. Decorate with ribbon, glitter, etc., for a decoration. (Makes a cute ornament for Christmas tree and a nice gift.)

- On nature walks collect items for study and use for nature collages.

- Paint stones or rocks or decorate.

- Use mesh net type fabric or other fabric scraps and fill with flower petals, potpourri or other herbs, then tie to make a sachet.

- Press flowers in plastic wrap with heavy book and then keep.

- Make leaf prints: collect leaves, lay thin newsprint on top, rub crayon over, the veins of leaves should stand out and you will have a leaf print.

- Experiment with different kinds of seeds. Plant and see differences in leaves, plants, where each grows best, etc. Use seeds for art collages also.

- Read *Jack and the Beanstalk*. Give child bean seeds to plant. Also, let him draw his own beanstalk on paper, glue seeds on it, and write story about what he might find at the top of the beanstalk.

- Collect pine cones. Decorate with paint or glitter for decorations. Use to make birdfeeders. Add small amount of peanut butter (birds can't really eat the peanut butter), and birdseed. Hang in tree. Also use pinecones and glue, paper or other items to make animals.

- Use old cornhusk and tie together to make doll. Use old sock or fabric scrap and fill with cotton, tie at top for head and attach to the cornhusk.

- Potato head doll: use potato and decorate as doll. Use toothpicks to attach parts, use other food items such as miniature marshmallows, raisins, etc. for parts or seeds, grass, flowers, etc. Make clothes out of small scraps of paper or fabric.

- Use fruits and vegetables and put together to make animals. Use orange slices, carrots, cucumber, etc. Use your imagination.

- The Voo doo Tube? To be or not to be; use with limits. Try to encourage educational programs. Allow some "fun" shows but not hours of couch potato time.

- Help your child learn to sew. Begin with simple projects. An apron, doll blankets or clothes, small pillows, etc., are good starts.

- Make up a musical, sing songs and record. Make up a show and invite friends.

- Make paper flowers from construction paper, tissue paper, or cupcake holders.

- Use stamps or small stencils to make note pads, decorate envelopes, wrapping paper, etc.

- Try different crafts: make rag dolls, create model cars, weaving, make paper and painted earrings, jewelry from beads, small stained glass paint projects, and a variety of other crafts which are available in craft stores.

- Make instruments from paper plates, pie pans or cans (fill with beans or seeds and glue edges together.) Make a microphone from a tube covered in aluminum foil. Use for speaking or singing.

- Make a large map or mural of the neighborhood.

- Tye dye shirts. Use regular tye dye method or fill squirt bottles with fabric paint diluted with water. Tie pieces of shirt with rubber bands and then squirt with paint.

- Make toy boats from bar of soap, straw and plastic. Use in bathtub.

- Try different ways of painting. String painting (dip string in paint, drag across paper to make designs, or fold paper with string in middle, press and pull string, open to see design.) Paint blots: put small amount of paint in middle of paper, fold paper, rub, open to see design. Give design a name. Fingerpaint with paint or pudding, then lick fingers clean. Blow paint; put small amounts of different colors of paint on paper, blow with straw to make designs and mix colors.

- Make thumbprints with paint or ink. Design to make picture or make a drawing out of each print.

- Try origami.

- Candy contest: fill jar with candy or small jars with different kinds of candy. Let children estimate how many pieces in jar. Then count, graph and eat a few. Save some for rewards.

- Watermelon: estimate how big around it is, measure, cut, eat, count seeds. Paint watermelon pictures on t-shirts. Use real seeds for artwork.

- Make a bug catcher out of jar and catch bugs. Get books from library and study different kinds of bugs.

- Styrofoam art: use small styrofoam peanuts and other scraps and glue on paper or stack to make a creation.

- Leather jar or vase: use small baby food jar or other jar. Cover with small torn pieces of masking tape. Buff with brown shoe polish. It resembles leather.

- Toothpick art: use colored toothpicks and let your child use his imagination to create a picture.

- Clothespin butterflies: use tissue paper or use coffee filter (fold and dip corners in food coloring), put between clothespin. Use pipecleaners for antenna.

- Make lotto game. Cut pictures from magazines and make up own game.

- Sponge paint: buy precut sponges or cut your own designs. Press in paint and decorate shirts, paper, hats, etc.

- Read *Harold and the Purple Crayon;* let your child draw with purple crayon and label " " and the Purple Crayon. Let them make up a story about the picture.

- Read *Green Eggs and Ham*; cook eggs and color green, eat! Do other "green" art that day. Paint with green paint, cut green paper and use for project. Do the same with other colors. For example, Red Day: read *Little Red Riding Hood.* Do "red" art.

- Read *Blueberries for Sal*, pick blueberries or buy some at the store and make a blueberry pie. Use small bottle tops, dip in blue paint and press on paper to make blueberry pictures.

- Vegetable print: cut potato or green pepper in half, cut design or shape out of potato and dip in paint. Print on paper.

- Design and decorate own placemats. Cover with clear contact paper.

- Make bookmarks from construction paper, decorate, cover with contact paper.

- Make bug collection. Paint big, beautiful, black, brown and blue bugs.

- Outside relay races: spoon races, egg toss, 3 leg races, sack races, water balloon toss, etc., are always hits. Have a field day in your neighborhood.

- Outside: play Duck Duck Goose, musical chairs, hot potato.

- Make paper chains: cut paper in various shapes and designs and then chain together. Make as necklace or decoration for room.

- Decorate sun visors, straw hats, other hats with paint, ribbon, craft items.

- Wooden spoon dolls: paint face on oval part of spoon, add yarn for hair, cloth or tissue clothes, straws for arms and legs, etc.

- Get a calendar and list one activity for each day on it. Make up your own ideas. Suggestions: read your favorite story to a friend. Then let them read to you. Go for a walk and see how many kinds of birds you can see. Write a story about baseball. Read the funny pages or cartoon section. Draw and make up your own cartoon character. Taste a fruit or vegetable that you've never tasted before. Cut words from a newspaper and make a sentence with them. Look for things that begin with a certain letter; for example, "M" or "B." Clean up your neighborhood. Draw a picture of things you do to cool off when you're hot. Build a stick birdhouse. Pretend you are a flower or a bug. Write about how you grow or what you would do. Make a tall sandwich. Measure it. Measure other things in the house. Make an autograph book for summer friends to share. Search your yard for caterpillars; read a book about a caterpillar such as *The Very Hungry Caterpillar.* Make a playhouse out of sticks and leaves. Pull five weeds. Count the leaves on each weed. Paint a picture of your back yard on a sunny day, then on a rainy or cloudy day. Create a new peanut butter treat or chocolate dessert. Carve a design, animal, boat, etc., out of a bar of soap.

- Make costumes out of paper bags or old pillow cases. Kids can decorate with magic markers, glue items on.

- Cooking: Cooking is fun, rewarding (you can eat your project), and a great learning experience. When cooking, you are teaching counting, measuring, consistencies, changes in form, language, sequencing, etc. Also emphasize cleanliness, safety in kitchen, and cleaning up after self. Kids can chop vegetables and fruits, measure ingredients, stir and pour, make sandwiches and desserts, make own lunches and picnics, make brownies, ice cakes, etc. Books with fun kid recipes are available in book stores and educational stores. Included are two fun recipes for summer.

## Dirt Dessert

Make vanilla or chocolate pudding. Layer with crushed oreo cookies, cool whip and pudding. Include gummie worms and serve in a clean plant pot (or paper cup).

## Sand Dessert

Mix vanilla pudding. Layer with cool whip and crushed vanilla wafers. Put shark bites in and serve in clean sand bucket with shovel.

**Art Recipes** (be sure to supervise, some are for eating, others are not, stress this)

### Peanut Butter Playdough

1 18 oz. jar peanut butter

6 tblsp. honey

non-fat dry milk

Combine peanut butter and honey. Add milk until proper consistency. Decorate the creation with raisins, nuts, etc.

### Frosting Fundough

1 can frosting mix

1 1/2 c. powdered sugar

1 cup peanut butter

Have children mix all ingredients until they form a workable dough.

### Cornstarch Magic

1/2 cup cornstarch

1/4 cup water

food coloring

a teaspoon and margarine tub

Place cornstarch into margarine tub. Slowly add water, 1 tsp. at a time, and stir. Feel the mixture with your hands. Continue adding water, 1 tsp. at a time until the mixture is a thick paste. Observe the changes in the mixture as you add water. Pick up the mixture and let it ooze through your fingers. Add 3 drops of food coloring, without mixing it in, and watch it disperse through the mixture. Also, put different colors of dough in a plastic zip lock bag and squeeze, then watch the colors mix.

## Uncooked Playdough

3 c. flour

1 c. salt

3 tblsp. baby oil

1 c. water

Mix dry ingredients together. Stir in oil and water. Add more water if needed to form a soft pliable dough.

## Cloud Dough

6 c. flour

1 c. salad oil

enough water to make pliable, food coloring if desired

This dough is very soft and elastic. It can be kept covered in container or plastic. Keeps one week.

## Oatmeal Dough

2 c. oatmeal

1 c. flour

1/2 c. water

Mix, create, let dry, paint.

## Volcano

1/4 c. vinegar

1/4 c. detergent

6 tblsp. bacon soda

food coloring

Put liquids in first. Put plaster of paris around jar. Pour liquid in.

### Magical Crystal Garden (from Craft Fun)

*Craft Fun* by Janet McCarty and Betty Peterson, published by Golden Press)

6 tblsp. salt

6 tblsp. water

6 tblsp. laundry bluing

1 tblsp. ammonia

food coloring

5-6 pieces charcoal

Mix salt, water, bluing and ammonia. Put charcoal in glass container. Pour mixture over charcoal. Sprinkle food coloring to give garden color. Set in warm place. Watch grow.

### Salt Goop (from *Craft Fun*)

4 c. flour

1 1/2 c. water

1 c. salt

Shape goop to make sculptures. Bake at 350 degrees for 1 hour.

### Sand or Salt Paint

Mix small amount of sand or salt with paint. Gives textured pictures. Another version is to put sand or salt (color with food coloring) in salt or pepper shaker and shake onto glue for design.

### Salt Paint

2 tsp. salt

1 tsp. liquid starch

1 tsp. water

few drops of tempera paint

Mix in bowl and paint; gives shiny grainy picture.

## LIE DOWN ON THE COUCH:
## THE PROS SPEAK

Couch potato or counseling? Whatever the reason, the couch is a comfortable place to be. Everyone wants a cozy comfortable place to curl up and vegetate at times. Everyone wants a cozy comfortable place to curl up and unload their inner feelings at times. Some families are able to meet all these needs at home, but sometimes, for some reason, you may need to seek help, advice, or just another ear to listen.

Pediatricians, counselors, psychologists, and psychiatrists are available if the need arises. Most schools have incorporated counselors into their programs. These counselors usually meet with students in their classes, in small groups, or individually upon request from a teacher, parent, or the child themselves. Schools often offer parenting seminars and classes throughout the course of a year. Churches also offer similar services, usually at a negotiable rate. If a problem occurs which needs more serious attention, private psychologists and psychiatrists may be your option.

Also, numerous parenting books can be found in book stores and libraries. A multitude of topics are presented from the general to the very detailed depending on your need. A list of suggested books for general use is found in the section titled "Additional Resources." Others are available for more detailed topics such as attention deficit disorders, speech impairments, gifted children, etc.

While some of the suggestions given in this chapter are specifically for the summer, a great deal of the advice can be used as good practical parenting year round. What do these pros have to say about school break? Well, lie down on the couch, get comfortable and read on.

## GENERAL SUGGESTIONS

- Provide unconditional love; acceptance of your child
- Praise positive behavior and efforts
- Promote a positive self concept
- Use positive reinforcement
- Spend quality time with your child
- Listen to your child
- To Spank or Not? Refer to *The Re-creation of a Nation through Real Parenting* by Michael J. Mayer, Ed.D.
- Use reflective listening
- Watch the stress level of your child. Seek help if needed
- Set limits and be consistent in following through
- Be a good role model

- Use time out method

- Utilize resources available: your library, bookstores and available books, parenting classes offered through local schools and churches, school counselors

### OTHER SUGGESTIONS:

(With permission, taken from handouts prepared by counselors at Pinckneyville Middle School; Mrs. DeBrody)

- Give children responsibilities. Pick a calendar and let the child choose what jobs he/she can do. Mark the days on the calendar with post it notes to indicate date needed for completion. Plan simple rewards such as swimming, inviting a friend over, etc.

- Ask your child to list five or six children he or she wants to become better friends with. Encourage them to invite one of the children for lunch, a picnic, etc.

- Encourage your child to be involved in large muscle sports activities: swimming, baseball, bowling, gymnastics, karate, etc.

- Allow your child to participate in cooking. Begin to teach responsibility in the kitchen, safety in cooking habits, planning and preparing meals.

- Do problem solving discussions. Try to monitor and guide TV watching. Encourage shows such as "The Wonder Years" and discuss the show afterwards. Ask your child to place himself in the position of the character. What would he/she do in that situation?

- If working on academic skills, limit to twenty minute intervals. Look for school supply workbooks. Breaking tasks into small amounts helps children feel a sense of accomplishment.

- Set a routine, schedule, and keep a little order to the day.

- Avoid letting the child get too dependent on you for his day. Encourage him to plan activities himself.

- Schedule summer memberships at YWCA or YMCA. These organizations offer camps and summer programs as well as babysitting classes.

- Look in local bookstores to see if a guide book for your city has been published. Often a specific book for a city may list activities for children in the area. If not, check the newspaper for listings.

- Use a Job Jar and Reward Jar. Kids make up jobs and rewards to go in each jar. Pick one job a day. Rewards: use a variety of rewards, not just money; for example; extra tv time, free job pass, time with family member of choice, lunch out, etc.

- A variation is a STAR JAR or CHART: make squares for each child. Sporadically give out stars as reward. Reward a variety of things: positive behaviors, if you see your child compliment or help someone, showing initiative around the house, not complaining, etc. When a child receives a certain number of stars, a bigger reward is given. Decide these in advance.

- Middle school age children develop a need for privacy and for this privacy to be respected. Parents should look at interactions with children and communicate more adult to adult. A series recommended and used by middle school counselors entitled *Active Parenting of Teens* focuses on the concept of a problem solving model. This concept encourages parents to put ownership of problems with a child onto the child. The parent doesn't own the child's problem. He may assist if truly necessary and be there for support, but the child should be encouraged to own and solve his own problems. Children become more motivated when it is personalized and they take ownership of their own problem.

- Problem Solving the **I DEAL** way means I Deal With Problems. A short written form for Problem Solving might be helpful. Write down the following and let the child answer, then act upon it.

## Step 1: Identify the problem

My problem is: _____

## Step 2: Describe what can be done

I could: _____

## Step 3: Evaluate what might happen; select the best answer

If I: _____

## Step 4: Act on best answer

My plan is to: _____

## Step 5: Learn if that helped

I'll know if I have a good solution if:_____

- A suggested method for helping families is the family meeting. At the family meeting, preferably weekly, the family meets to discuss schedules for the week, plans, needs, problems, etc. Hopefully, by discussing in advance and ironing out details of plans for the week, expectations, jobs, etc., parents and children can avoid some of the rushed mistakes and confrontations that occur in their busy lives. Also, at the family meeting, children and parents can both set goals for the week. At the next family meeting, each can discuss whether they obtained these goals and set new ones.

- Encourage middle school age children and teens to take responsibility for money. Teens can work at summer jobs. Middle school age children can do odd jobs or service oriented jobs and find ways to help in the community. Encourage your middle schooler to make up his own flyer for odd jobs; suggestions are pet sitting, picking up mail while a family is on vacation, cut grass, yardwork, babysit, organize photos and put into albums, wash cars, clean house, etc.

# CHAPTER 8

## FAMOUS LAST WORDS

"Freedom at last
Freedom at last
Freedom at last!"

The famous words of Martin Luther King or moms at the bus stop on the first day of school?

Certainly a sigh of relief and joy mixed with new anxiety over the upcoming year filters thru your body as you watch your children climb the steps for a new year. You realize that once a parent you're always a parent and that your freedom is a bygone commodity. With each stage of growth and change comes a new set of worries and problems.

Other famous words haunt you as you hear the rhythm of the screeching school bus approaching:

- "It's better to have loved and lost than never to have loved at all."
- "Jesus loves the little children, all the children of the world. Red and yellow, black and white, they are precious in his sight. Jesus loves the little children of the world."
- "Trick or treat, smell my feet, give me something good to eat. If you don't, I don't care, I'll pull down your underwear."
- "Mom, he's looking at me!"
- "Nanny nanny boo boo, stick your head in _____."

Then another set of famous last words brings you back to reality, "Mom, I gotta go to the bathroom!" You snatch her hand and race her back to the house as you hear the bus on the other street. "Hurry up," you remind her, "You're going to miss the bus."

## PAT YOURSELF ON THE BACK: THE SCHOOL BUS IS ROLLING AROUND THE CORNER

"The wheels on the bus go round and round, round and round, round. The wheels on the bus go round and round all around the town." Well, you've almost made it! Pat yourself on the back, the school bus is right around the corner. Another long hot summer survived. The children have their new bookbags, school supplies, and new school shoes (you're trying to block the cost of all that from your mind). You've met the new teachers (another anxiety attack passed or possibly the beginning depending on your impression) and you notice a slight bit of excitement in your kids' eyes as they talk of seeing old friends.

The night before school you find yourself restless, tossing in your sleep, and to your own surprise twinges of sadness creep in. The hurry scurry of the first morning, "Do I look okay in this?," "Mom, that's not the style in third grade!," "I can't get my hair to do right," keeps everyone too busy to think.

As you stand waiting at the bus stop, camera in hand for the yearly picture, a tear drop unexpectedly appears in the corner of your eye. You quickly swipe it with your sleeve but suddenly anticipation for the new year climbs all the way up your back and grabs you by the earlobes. You long for those lazy days of summer, sitting blissfully by the pool, spending time with your kids, the wonderful vacation at the beach, long long walks and bike rides, everyone sitting at the table eating and sharing conversation. What a great summer, you think.

The bus looks huge as it roars around the corner. Will the kids like the bus driver this year and their new teacher? Will they make new friends or forget how to go their classroom? Their feet shrink sizes as they climb the dark stairs and you see tiny hands wave timidly to you, a wondering trusting face pressed against the window. That wasn't a tear in his eyes, was it? You quickly shove that thought into the crevices of your mind and biting your lip, you force a big smile and wave. The long yellow bus chugs out of sight and you stand motionless for a moment in time.

Feelings swirl inside you like the ingredients in a blender.

Perhaps you cheer and chant, "Yes, yes, Baby!"then breathe a sigh of relief. Perhaps you sob a little melancholy baby.

Perhaps you're off to a job or have planned a fun day for yourself. Afterall, you deserve it. This is your time. Perhaps you face the empty house, so quiet after the months (or years) of noisy children and friends, messy rooms, meals, laundry.

The telephone rings. You hear your neighbor's voice. "Did you cry or are you celebrating?" you ask your neighbor.

"Well, Julie's mom has been crying her eyes out all morning, but I've waited thirteen years for this last one to go to school," the other voice says, "I'm celebrating! I told my husband not to dare come home for lunch today. This is the first day I've had to myself in years."

A day to yourself, what will you do? You automatically bend to collect the toys left on the floor and the clothes shoved into the corner while you carry the portable phone under your ear. You think about how you can keep the house neat and tidy. Become an obsessive cleaner? No, you decide.

"Well, you know I might even read a book or go to a movie," your neighbor continues to chatter. "I'm going to give myself two weeks, then tackle all those projects I've been putting off. Oh, look at the clock. Boy, does time fly. I've got to go. Bye!"

Time does fly. Where did all the days go? They went so fast. If you only had one more week, you think. All the unmet goals for the summer race across your mind, the times you were cross, the cuddly times on the sofa. Then you start to hum, "Where have all the flowers gone?"

---

## "WHERE HAVE ALL THE FLOWERS GONE, LONG TIME PASSING?"

*by Pete Seger*

In your mind, the song echoes over and over:

"Where have all the flowers gone, long time passing?
Where have all the flowers gone, long time ago?
Where have all the flowers gone?
Young girls pick them everyone,
Oh when will they ever learn.

Where have all the young girls gone, long time passing?
Where have all the young girls gone, long time ago?
Where have all the young girls gone?
Gone to young men everyone.

Where have all the young men gone, long time passing?
Where have all the young men gone, long time ago?
Where have all the young men gone?
Gone to soldiers everyone.

Where have all the soldiers gone, long time passing?
Where have all the soldiers gone, long time ago?
Where have all the soldiers gone?
Gone to graveyards everyone.

Where have all the graveyards gone, long time passing?
Where have all the graveyards gone, long time ago?
Where have all the graveyards gone?
Gone to flowers everyone."

As the song echoes in your mind, you realize and remind yourself that one day, your kids will roll around the corner for their own homes, their own destinations, their own dreams, their own lives. A moment you've lived for and have longed for. Or have you? Or have you lived for the day and the moments and treasured them as you made them. The smart person you are, you have made plans for yourself when the children are gone, whether it is just to school or for their own roads in life. Yes, remember that person underneath is still there and with all the love and time you have for your kids, you also have that love and now some time for yourself. The road may have been bumpy and filled with detours and potholes but, yes, pat yourself on the back, you made it, a job well done!

"Know that in all the beauty of the flower
it too shall pass
yet transcend through time
and though the flower may wilt without love and care
it will grow and adorn the world with beauty
when it is adorned itself."

# ADDITIONAL SUGGESTED RESOURCES

Listed are a few additional resources. Others are found, depending on your interest, in educational and teacher supply stores as well as some local bookstores, libraries, and craft stores.

**Arts and Crafts**

Sunset, *Crafts for Children*

Instructor's *Artfully Easy!*

Highlights *Creative Craft Activities*

*Puppets* by Mabel Duch (A Good Apple Activity Book)

*Balloon Bonanza* by Hope Joyce (Teacher Created Materials)

Monday Morning Series, *Gift Crafts, Crafts* by Jean Warren

Fearon Series, *Great Gifts for All Occasions, Mother Goose Paper Crafts, Folk Tale Paper Crafts, Pinwheels, Pop-ups and Puppets*

**Cooking**

*Book Cooks*

Better Homes and Gardens; *Kids' Snacks*

*Cooking - Picture Recipes* by Barbara Johnson

**Nature and Science**

*Exciting Things to do With Nature Materials* by Judy Allen

The Table Top Learning Series: *Science Fun, Rainbow Fun, Backyard, Rainy Day, Cookbook*

*50 Simple Things Kids Can Do to Save the Earth by* The Earthworks Group

*Using Recyclables for Arts and Crafts*

## Magazines

Child Magazine

Humpty Dumpty magazine for children

Highlights for Children

Peanut Butter Magazine

Lollipops Magazine

Teacher

Learning

Instructor

Parenting

## Newsletter

*Growing Together, Growing Child(birth-6 years), Growing Up (grades K-12)* This newsletter is published by Dunn & Hargitt, Inc., Lafayette, In.  47902-1100, 1-800-388-2624

## Books on Child Raising and Discipline

*The Re-Creation of a Nation through REAL PARENTING by* Michael J. Mayer, Ed.D.

*Character Development Encouraging Self-Esteem & Self-Discipline in Infants, Toddlers and Two Year Olds by* Polly Greenberg

*Toddlers & Parents by* T. Berry Brazelton, M.D.

*The Parent's Handbook by* Don Dinkmeyer and Gary P. McKay

*You & Your Child's Self Esteem by* James M. Harris, Ph.D.

A series of books by Dr. Fitzhugh Dodson; two suggestions are:

*How to Parent* and *How to Discipline With Love*

Three suggestions by Adele Faber and Elaine Maylish are:

*How to Be the Parent You Always Wanted to Be*

*Siblings Without Rivalry*

*How to Talk So Kids Will Listen, & Listen So Kids Will Talk*

Two books by Rudolf Dreikurs, M.D. with Vicki Soltz, R.N. are:

*The Challenge of Parenthood*

*Children: The Challenge*

*The First Five Years of Life, The Child From Five to Ten, and Youth: The Years From 10-16* by Arnold Gesell

## OTHER

**The Everything Book** by Valerie Indenbaum and Marcia Shapiro

*Things to Do With Toddlers and Twos* by Karen Miller

Playworks series; *Artworks, Gameworks, Constructions, Contraptions, Toyworks*

*Parent Tricks of the Trade* by Kathleen Town

*Motherhood Stress* by Deborah Shaw Lewis

*KIDS' U.S. ROAD ATLAS*, a Backseat Book from Rand McNally

*VACATION BOOK* by Deri Robins, published by Mallard Press

*365 TV-Free Activities You Can Do With Your Child* by Steve & Ruth Bennett

*A Mother's Manual for Summer Survival* by Kathy Peel and Joy Mahaffey

*Trouble-Free Travel with Children* by Vicki Lansky

*Thinking Games to Play With Your Child* by Cheryl Tuttle and Penny Paquette

*Hey! Listen to This* (Stories to Read Aloud) Edited by Jim Trelease

On Audio Cassette: Valentine Productions Fairy Game Mother Series;

*Games for the Road, More Games for the Road, Games for Birthday Parties, Games for Rainy Days* available though Deborah Valentine, Valentine Productions, 3856 Grand Forest Dr., Norcross, GA. 30092

# MOM'S SUMMER JOURNAL

**FUN SUMMER ACTIVITIES**

**PLACES TO VISIT**

**OUR VACATION**

**TRAVEL ACTIVITIES**

## FAVORITE GAMES

## FAVORITE RAINY DAY ACTIVITIES

## FAVORITE MUSEUMS

## PLACES WHICH OFFER CHILDREN'S PROGRAMS OR DISCOUNTS

## WAYS I ORGANIZED WORK AND JOB CHARTS

## IDEAS THAT WORK

## IDEAS THAT DIDN'T WORK

## SPORTS ACTIVITIES I ENJOYED

**BOOKS I READ**

**GOALS I SET**

**GOALS I REACHED**

**NEW FRIENDS I MADE**

# MY SUMMER VACATION

## BY

**GOALS I SET:**

**GOALS I COMPLETED:**

**NEW FRIENDS I MADE:**

**OLD FRIENDS I KEPT:**

**OUR VACATION:**

**MOST FUN SUMMER ACTIVITIES**

**PLACES TO VISIT**

**THINGS I DID WHEN WE TRAVELED**

**FAVORITE INSIDE GAMES**

**FAVORITE OUTSIDE GAMES**

**FAVORITE RAINY DAY ACTIVITIES**

**FAVORITE MOVIES**

**FAVORITE MUSEUMS**

**OTHER PLACES WE VISITED**

## JOBS I DID

## WAYS I EARNED MONEY

## SPORTS ACTIVITIES I ENJOYED

## BOOKS I READ

Dear Mom,

Thanks for a great summer!

We Love You!

Your Kids!

# OTHER FINE BOOKS FROM R&E ! ! !

**SURVIVING SUMMERS WITH KIDS: Fun Filled Activities for All by Rita B. Herron.** It comes every year, inexorably like death and taxes, the dreaded summer break. When schools close, parents are at the mercy of their unoccupied and restless children. This light-hearted, easy-to-read book is filled with anecdotes and tips for surviving summer vacations with your psyche intact. Written by a teacher and mother.

$9.95                                                                    ISBN 1-56875-052-8
Soft Cover                                                               Order #052-8

---

**THE ABC'S OF PARENTING: Keep Your Kids in Touch and Out of Trouble by Joan Barbuto.** Raising children in our society is more difficult than ever before. This book gives parents the practical tools they need to raise responsible, capable and well-adjusted children. It teaches parents the 20 rules of discipline they must know and apply and how to avoid the types of discipline that are ineffective and psychologically damaging.

$14.95                                                                   ISBN 1-56875-062-5
Soft Cover                                                               Order #062-5

---

**TAKING CHARGE: A Parent and Teacher Guide to Loving Discipline by Jo Anne Nordling.** At last, here is a book that shows both parents and teachers everything they need to know to discipline children effectively and fairly.

This easy-to-understand action guide will show you how to handle the most critical disciplinary issues in teaching and raising children.

$11.95                                                                   ISBN 0-88247-906-7
Trade Paper                                                              Order #9906-7

---

**TALKING JUSTICE: 602 Ways to Build & Promote Racial Harmony by Tamera Trotter & Jocelyn Allen.** It is said that a journey of a thousand miles begins with a single step. This important new book is a map to the small steps that each of us can take on the path to ending prejudice and hatred. We can use these methods to bridge the gap that exists between us and members of other races. With each small, tenuous action we take, we are that much closer to understanding each other.

This simple yet profound guide is ideal for teachers, clergy and individuals who want to end the hatred and venture into a strange, but beautiful new land of harmony and cooperation.

$6.95                                                                    ISBN 0-88247-982-2
Soft Cover                                                               Order #982-2

**BECOMING THE ME I WANT TO BE: A Self-Help Guide to Building Self-Esteem by Don G. Simmermacher.** Everything that you do in life, from the amount of money you make to the person you marry, is determined by your self-esteem and self-image. It is believed that most of us use less than 10% of our true potential, and that if we learned how to tap into it we could transform our lives. This book will help you discover and develop a more powerful sense of self to help change your life dramatically.

$9.95                ISBN 1-56875-055-2                Order #055-2

---

**THE POWER OF POSITIVE EDUCATION by Will Clark.** Our education system is failing our children. It is not preparing them to succeed in a world which is growing increasingly more complex and demanding. Instead of helping children to become motivated learners, we are teaching them to be irresponsible and destructive. This book offers a new model and a new hope. It teaches parents, educators, political and business leaders how to work together to provide our children with the education they need and deserve.

$9.95                ISBN 1-56875-057-9                Order #057-9

---

**WHAT IS HAPPENING TO OUR CHILDREN: How to Raise them Right by Mardel Gustafson.** Here is a book that will help parents to restore some old-fashioned values in our children. It is time, the author believes, for women to return to the most important job of all—raising their children. Only in this way will the strength of the family be restored. With this stronger parental influence, children can be taught the values that will make them responsible citizens and have the strength to stay off of drugs and alcohol. Written by a former teacher and Sunday school instructor.

$7.95                ISBN 1-56875-044-7                Order #044-7